# The Wonders Inside
# BUGS
# & SPIDERS

# The Wonders Inside
# BUGS
# & SPIDERS

Silver Dolphin
San Diego, California

**Silver Dolphin Books**
An imprint of the Advantage Publishers Group
10350 Barnes Canyon Road, San Diego, CA 92121
www.silverdolphinbooks.com

Conceived and produced by Weldon Owen Pty Ltd
59–61 Victoria Street, McMahons Point
Sydney NSW 2060, Australia

ISBN-13: 978-1-57145-907-7
ISBN-10: 1-57145-907-3

Color reproduction by Chroma Graphics (Overseas) Pte Ltd
Printed by SNP Leefung Printers Ltd
Manufactured in China
1 2 3 4 5   13 12 11 10 09

A WELDON OWEN PRODUCTION

**BONNIER BOOKS**
**Group Publisher** John Owen

**WELDON OWEN PTY LTD**
**Chief Executive Officer** Sheena Coupe
**Creative Director** Sue Burk
**Publisher** Margaret Whiskin
**Senior Vice President, International Sales** Stuart Laurence
**Vice President, Sales: United States and Canada** Amy Kaneko
**Vice President, Sales: Asia and Latin America** Dawn Low
**Administration Manager, International Sales** Kristine Ravn
**Production Manager** Todd Rechner
**Production Coordinators** Lisa Conway, Mike Crowton

**Project Editor** Erin O'Brien
**Author** Jan Stradling
**Consultant** Dr. Noel Tait
**Designers** Sarah Norton, Kathryn Morgan
**Art Manager** Trucie Henderson

*Caterpillars' powerful jaws can cut through tough leaves.*

# CONTENTS

● Things with Wings   ● Bugs   ● Spiders   ● Beetles   ● About Insects   ● Layers

# WHAT IS AN INSECT?

Insects belong to a group of animals called arthropods. Instead of having bones inside their bodies like other animals, arthropods have a shell on the outside. This hard shell is called the exoskeleton. An insect's body is divided into three parts called the head, the thorax, and the abdomen. In the head are the brain, eyes, mouthparts, and two antennae. Six legs and the wings are attached to the thorax. The abdomen contains the insect's digestive and reproductive organs, and sometimes a stinger.

Spiders, crabs, scorpions, centipedes, ticks, and mites are arthropods but they are not insects. They are all different from insects in some way—spiders, scorpions, and ticks have eight legs and centipedes can have up to 400.

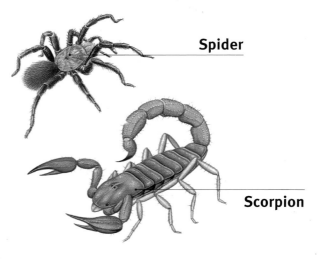

**Spider**

**Scorpion**

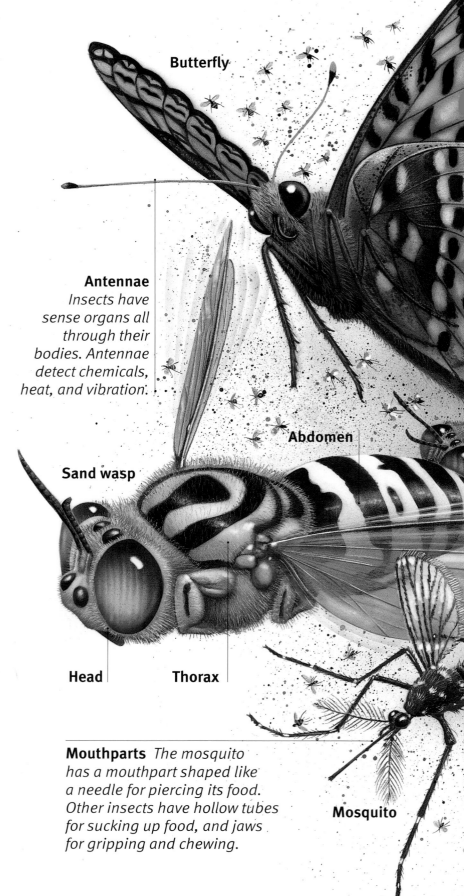

**Butterfly**

**Antennae** *Insects have sense organs all through their bodies. Antennae detect chemicals, heat, and vibration.*

**Abdomen**

**Sand wasp**

**Head**    **Thorax**

**Mouthparts** *The mosquito has a mouthpart shaped like a needle for piercing its food. Other insects have hollow tubes for sucking up food, and jaws for gripping and chewing.*

**Mosquito**

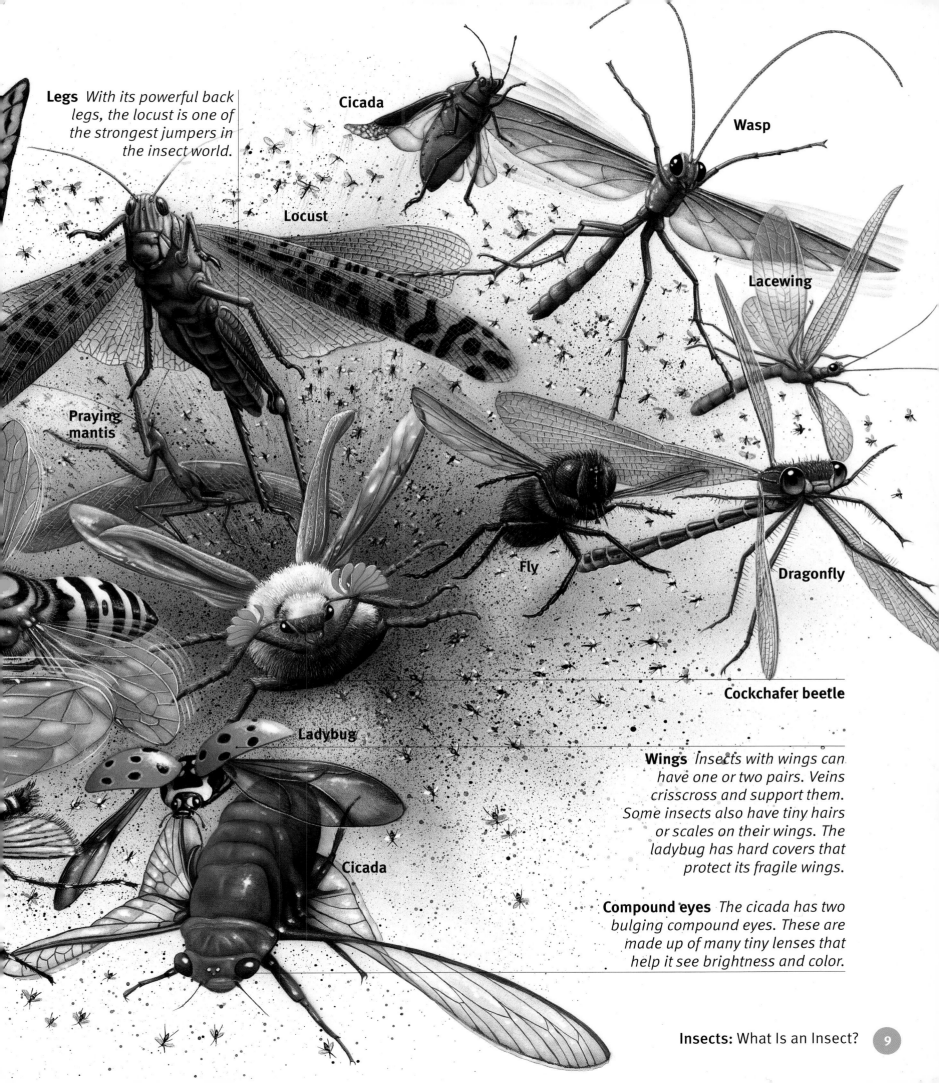

**Legs** With its powerful back legs, the locust is one of the strongest jumpers in the insect world.

Cicada

Wasp

Locust

Lacewing

Praying mantis

Fly

Dragonfly

Ladybug

Cockchafer beetle

Cicada

**Wings** Insects with wings can have one or two pairs. Veins crisscross and support them. Some insects also have tiny hairs or scales on their wings. The ladybug has hard covers that protect its fragile wings.

**Compound eyes** The cicada has two bulging compound eyes. These are made up of many tiny lenses that help it see brightness and color.

**Jaws** *Caterpillars need to eat all the time. Their powerful jaws can cut through tough leaves.*

**Head**

**Horns** *Insects and birds feed on caterpillars. This caterpillar has "horns" to scare off these enemies. When it is threatened, the caterpillar rears up to show its horns.*

**Thorax**

# CATERPILLARS

All insects begin life as an egg. When they hatch out, they have soft bodies and no wings and are called larvae. The larvae of butterflies and moths are known as caterpillars. Caterpillars have three pairs of legs on their thorax and five pairs of prolegs. Prolegs are not proper legs, but more like small stumps. Caterpillars feed nonstop and shed their skin several times as they grow. After some time, caterpillars need to pupate to become adults. During pupation, the caterpillar forms a hard protective coating around its body called a cocoon. The larva inside, which is now called a pupa, develops into an adult butterfly or moth and finally breaks out of the cocoon. This process is called complete metamorphosis and takes two to four weeks.

Many insects go through complete metamorphosis. Fly larvae are called maggots and beetle larvae are called grubs.

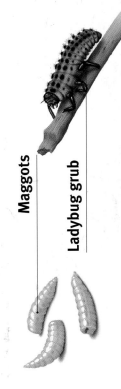

**Maggots**

**Ladybug grub**

# METAMORPHOSIS

**Page 12** *The caterpillar hatches from its egg and feeds constantly. It sheds its skin many times before it grows to full size.*

**Page 13** *After the caterpillar sheds its skin for the last time, it makes a cocoon in which to pupate—it is now a pupa. A butterfly pupa is called a chrysalis.*

**Eggs**

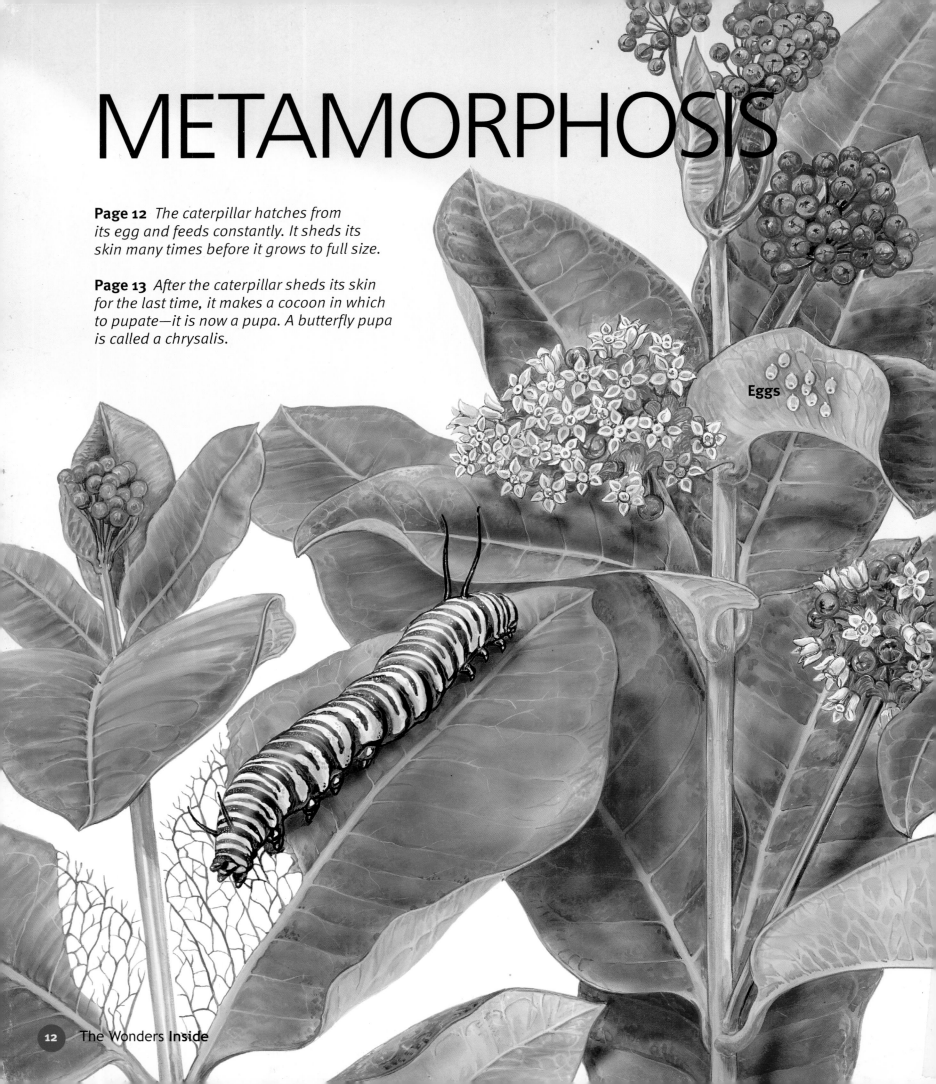

**Page 14** *Eventually the butterfly breaks out of its cocoon and clings to the empty shell. Blood is pumped into the wings to unfold them. They then become dry and flat and ready for flight.*

**Page 15** *Finally, the fully formed butterfly is able to fly away.*

# BUTTERFLIES AND MOTHS

Butterflies and moths have many things in common. They both go through metamorphosis. They both have a proboscis, which is a tube they use like a straw to suck up their food. They both also have two pairs of wings: front wings and back wings. But there are also some differences. A butterfly's antennae have knobs on the ends and a moth's do not. Butterflies are usually brightly colored and fly during the day. Moths are generally dull in color and fly at night.

**Color** *Brightly colored wing patterns help butterflies recognize one another and scare off enemies.*

**Tiger moth**

Butterflies rest with their wings upright. Moths rest with their wings flat.

**Marine blue butterfly**

**Feet** *A butterfly can taste with its feet.*

**Antennae** *Butterflies use these sense organs to smell, find their way, and balance.*

**Front wing**

**Back wing**
*Swallowtails get their name because of the long tail on each back wing, which is shaped like the tail of a bird called a swallow.*

**Eyespot** *Many butterflies and moths have a spot on their wings. These spots look like eyes and make the wings look like the face of a much bigger animal. This scares away attackers.*

# BUTTERFLY MIMIC

The colors and patterns of butterflies and moths are important for their survival. One of the best ways for a butterfly or moth to warn off an attacker is to copy, or mimic, a dangerous animal. The heliconid mimic butterfly looks identical to the poisonous heliconid butterfly. So, although it is harmless, birds leave it alone.

**Wing scales** *Tiny scales on a butterfly's wing reflect light and produce their brilliant colors. The scales are so small we cannot see them.*

**Heliconid mimic butterfly**

Insects use bright colors, like red, orange, and yellow, to warn off attackers. The warning colors and spots on these insects tell their attackers they taste bad.

**Five-spotted ladybug**

**Five-spotted Burnet moth**

**Ten-spotted ladybug**

**Flower attractions**
*Brightly colored flowers lure insects to their food. Insects can see colors that we cannot.*

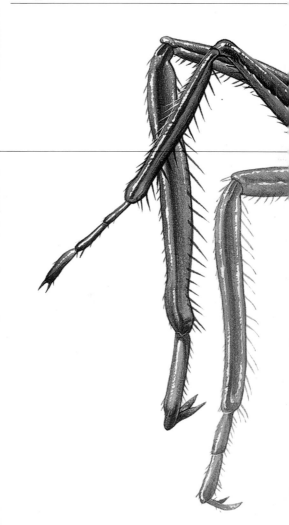

# DRAGONFLIES

The dragonfly is an aggressive hunter. It has powerful mouthparts and very strong, transparent wings. It is faster than any other insect, can fly backward, and can come to a sudden stop and hover like a helicopter. It preys on flying insects, which it catches in midair. It has two large compound eyes, which are made from 28,000 tiny lenses. These compound eyes let the dragonfly look in every direction at once. In addition to the compound eyes, it has three simple eyes that it uses for balance.

**Compound eye**
*Each one of the thousands of lenses gives the dragonfly a different view.*

**Simple eye**  *Three simple eyes on top of its head help the dragonfly to fly straight.*

## Inside info

Most insects, including bees, butterflies, and moths, flap both pairs of wings at the same time. Others, like beetles, flap only the back pair. Flies have only one pair of wings.

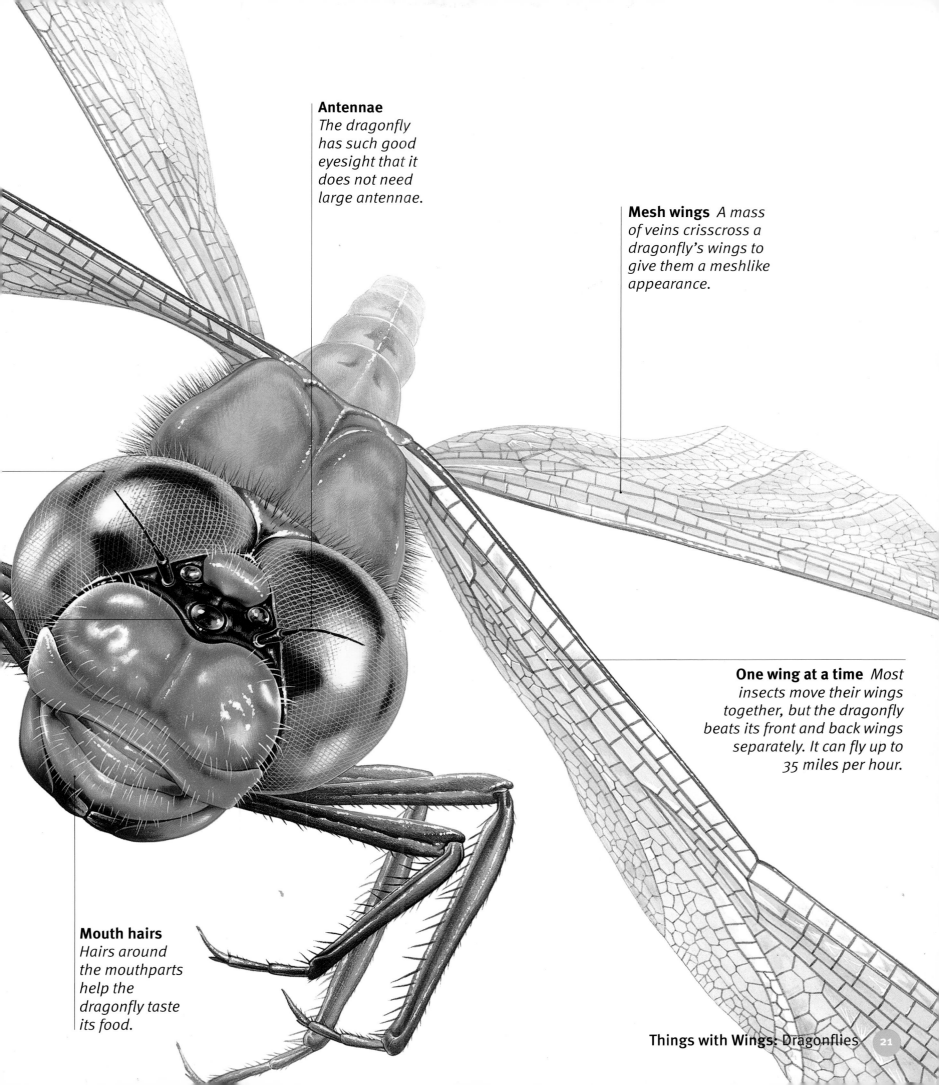

**Antennae**
*The dragonfly has such good eyesight that it does not need large antennae.*

**Mesh wings** *A mass of veins crisscross a dragonfly's wings to give them a meshlike appearance.*

**One wing at a time** *Most insects move their wings together, but the dragonfly beats its front and back wings separately. It can fly up to 35 miles per hour.*

**Mouth hairs**
*Hairs around the mouthparts help the dragonfly taste its food.*

# NYMPH TO ADULT

A dragonfly does not go through complete metamorphosis in the same way as some other insects, like moths and butterflies. It hatches from its egg as a nymph, which looks like a young adult dragonfly. The nymph is much smaller than its parent, does not have wings, and is usually a different color. As the nymph grows, it sheds its skin, or molts, many times before it reaches adult size. When the nymph molts for the last time, it breaks out of its old skin as a fully grown adult with wings. Even though adult dragonflies live in the air, their nymphs develop underwater. A dragonfly nymph can live underwater for as long as five years.

Other insects that hatch from eggs as nymphs include earwigs and locusts.

**Earwig nymph**

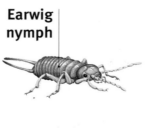

**Earwig adult**

**Locust nymph**

**Locust adult**

**The eggs** *Dragonflies either insert their eggs into a water plant, or let them fall to the bottom.*

**Hatched** *After a few weeks, the nymphs hatch from their eggs.*

**Final shed** *The dragonfly bursts from its old skin and is now a fully grown adult.*

**Adult dragonflies on the hunt**

**Mating** *A male and female mate and the eggs are fertilized.*

**Leaving** *The nymph climbs up a plant and out of the water before its final molt.*

**Nymph food** *A dragonfly nymph catches tadpoles and worms to eat.*

**Drying out** *The new adult dries its wings in the sunshine so they can fully expand.*

# DEERFLIES

Flies are the only flying insects that have one pair of wings. Instead of a second pair, they have small, club-shaped knobs. These are called halteres and are used for balance. An insect can fly because of powerful muscles in its thorax. Each wing is connected to the thorax by a tiny joint that allows the wing to move in many directions. The deerfly can beat its wings about 200 times per second—not as fast as a midge, which beats its wings at about 1,000 times per second.

**Upstroke** *At the top of the upstroke, the deerfly's wings are raised.*

**Downstroke** *Wing edges dip at the beginning of the downstroke.*

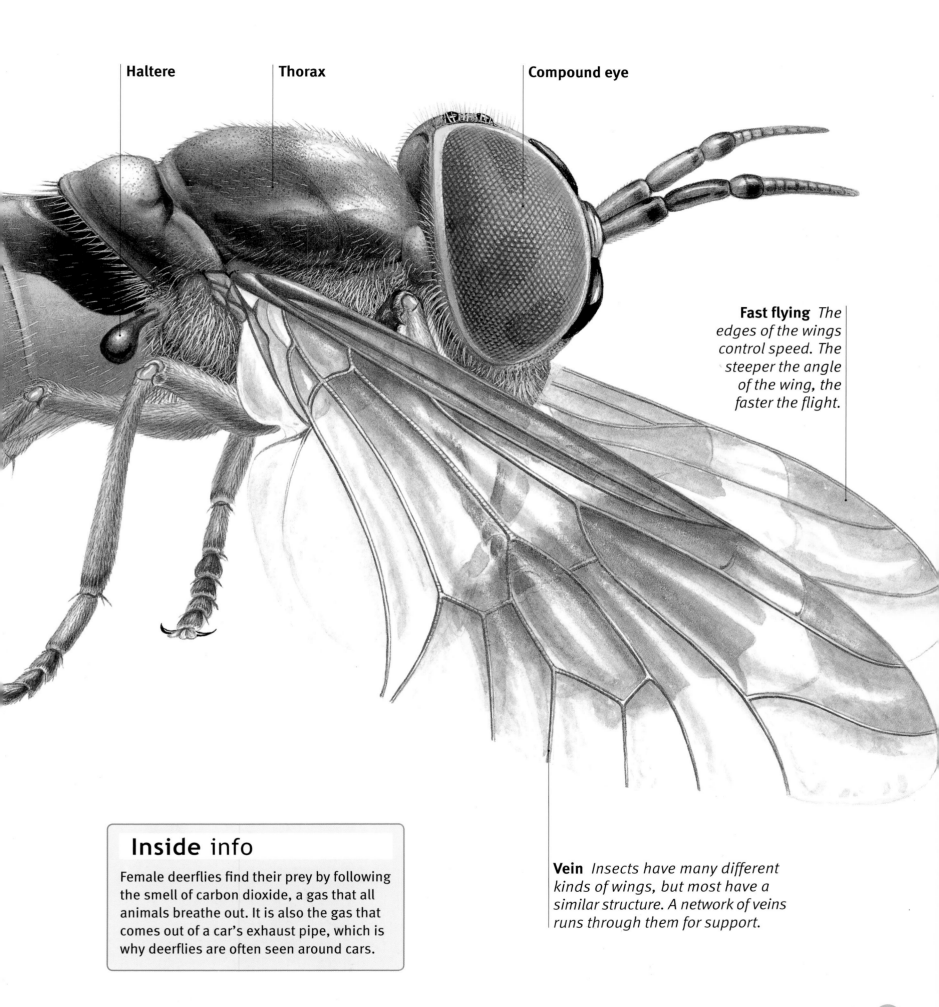

**Haltere**

**Thorax**

**Compound eye**

**Fast flying**  *The edges of the wings control speed. The steeper the angle of the wing, the faster the flight.*

## Inside info

Female deerflies find their prey by following the smell of carbon dioxide, a gas that all animals breathe out. It is also the gas that comes out of a car's exhaust pipe, which is why deerflies are often seen around cars.

**Vein**  *Insects have many different kinds of wings, but most have a similar structure. A network of veins runs through them for support.*

# BEEHIVE

**Queen bee**

**Page 26** *Bees live and work together as a group, or colony, within a beehive. Different kinds of bees perform different duties inside the hive. The single queen bee produces up to 2,500 eggs each day, and worker bees bring nectar and pollen back to the hive to feed the whole colony.*

**Page 27** *Honey is stored to feed the colony. The queen bee lays a single egg into each cell of the beehive.*

**Worker bee**

**Worker bee**

**Drone**

**Nurse worker**

**Page 28** *When the larva becomes a pupa, the top of the cell is sealed with wax. The pupa eventually becomes an adult bee.*

**Page 29** *It is the drones' job to fertilize the queen's eggs. The nurse worker makes honey from nectar to feed the growing larvae.*

# HOVERFLIES

There are about 120,000 species of flies, which include midges, mosquitoes, houseflies, and hoverflies. They range in size from a tiny dot to more than 3 inches long. The smallest fly in the world is the fairy fly, which is the size of the period at the end of this sentence. The hoverfly got its name because it can hover and dart among flowers and it can fly backward. Hoverflies usually have yellow stripes or spots to make them look like wasps and scare off attackers. If they are caught, they pretend to sting like a wasp, but they are harmless.

The hairy bee fly has a mouthpart like a tube, which is called a proboscis. It uses this to suck nectar out of flowers. Its proboscis can be three times longer than its head. Bee flies look like bumblebees and hover over their food.

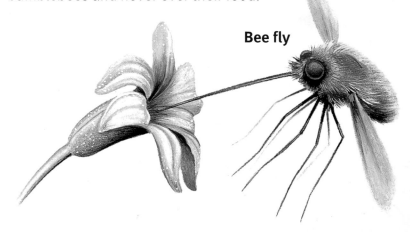

**Bee fly**

**Attracting a mate**
*A male hoverfly tries to attract a female by hovering above her.*

**Hovering around**
*Hoverflies keep their heads completely still when flapping their wings. After hovering like this, they can suddenly dart forward or sideways.*

All insects have two antennae, which come in different shapes and sizes. Many insects have poor eyesight and use their antennae to tell them what is happening around them.

**Weevil** *Uses its thin antennae to sense whether it has found food or a good place to lay eggs.*

**Male emperor moth** *Large featherlike antennae can pick up the scent of a female from more than 2 miles away.*

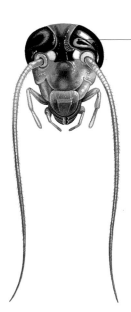

**Cockroach** *Most cockroaches live in dark places, so sight is not useful to them. Their long antennae can detect movement and smell food.*

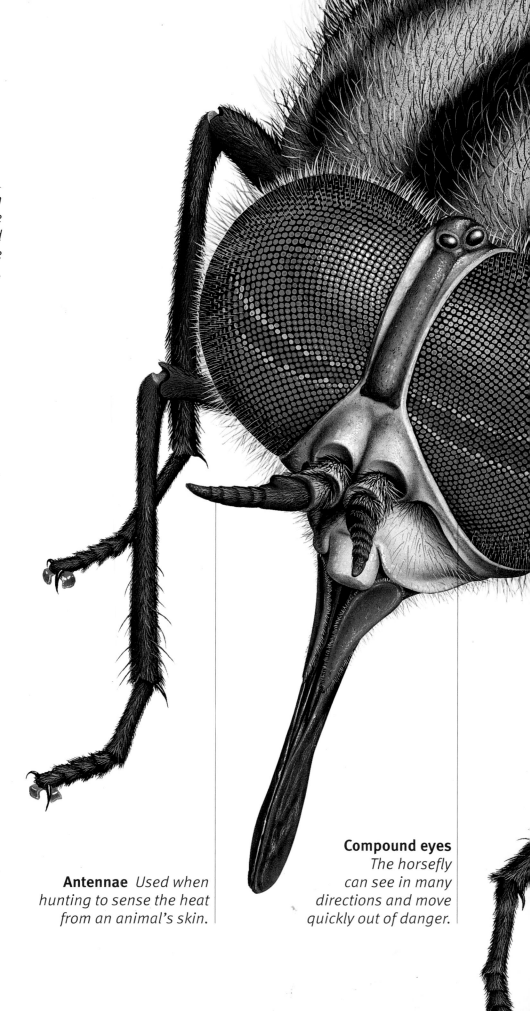

**Antennae** *Used when hunting to sense the heat from an animal's skin.*

**Compound eyes** *The horsefly can see in many directions and move quickly out of danger.*

# HORSEFLIES

Insects see, smell, taste, touch, and hear, but insect senses are very different from human senses. Insects have three main types of sensors that detect movement, smells, or light. They use their senses to find food, find a mate, and escape danger. The huge compound eyes of the horsefly give it powerful eyesight. This insect hunts for prey only in the daytime when it is light. Female horseflies feed on the blood of animals. They have strong mouthparts that let them bite through thick animal skin. Male horseflies do not have strong mouthparts, so instead of feeding on animals, they eat nectar.

**Feet** *Sticky pads on a fly's feet allow it to walk upside down. It can also taste with its feet.*

# ANT ATTACK

Hunting ants work together to attack and kill their prey. They attack their victims from all sides with their stingers. Then some ants use their jaws to pin down their prey, while others break it into tiny pieces and carry this food back to the nest. A single ant can lift up to 50 times its own body weight. So when ants work as a team, they can catch prey much larger than themselves, such as grasshoppers.

Every ant nest has its own smell. When these two red ants meet, they touch their antennae together to smell each other. In this way, they can tell if they are from the same nest.

## Inside info

The most dangerous ant is the black bulldog ant. It lives in Australia and can sting and bite at the same time.

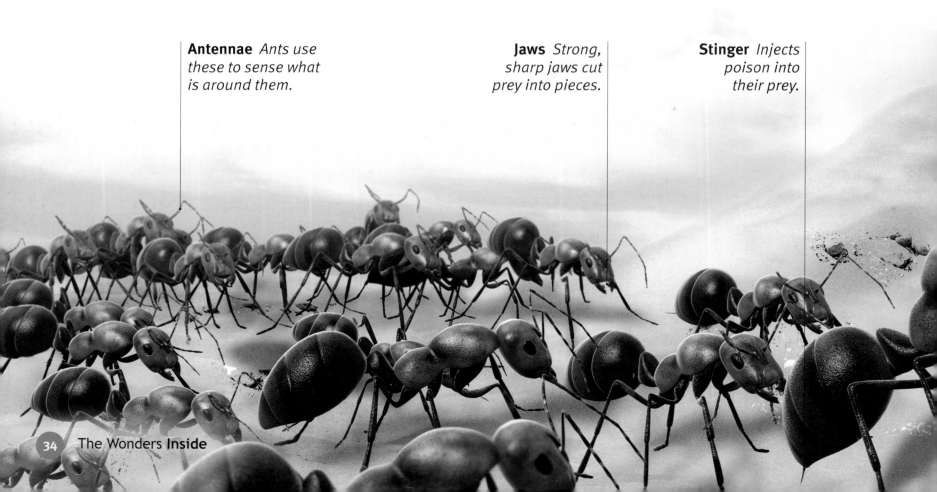

**Antennae** *Ants use these to sense what is around them.*

**Jaws** *Strong, sharp jaws cut prey into pieces.*

**Stinger** *Injects poison into their prey.*

Like all insects, ants have three body sections, three pairs of legs, and a pair of antennae.

**Head** *Holds the brain, antennae, eyes, and jaws.*

**Thorax** *The legs attach to this part of the body.*

**Abdomen** *Holds the internal organs, venom, and the stinger.*

# WASPS

**Page 36** *Wasps are attracted to the nectar and pollen in the center of flowers.*

**Page 37** *This is what a wasp looks like inside, without the exoskeleton. The wasp has different systems in its body, just like other animals. The breathing system is shown in light blue; the system for digesting food is green; the tubular heart is red; and the nervous system, including the brain, is dark blue.*

**Page 38** *This is what the wasp looks like with the yellow and black exoskeleton.*

**Page 39** *This is how the world may appear to a wasp—it can see colors that humans cannot. To a wasp, the flower has more detail than humans can see—and it may even guide the wasp to its pollen.*

**Queen** *Large with a huge abdomen, the queen's job is to lay eggs.*

**Male** *Small in size and sometimes with wings, males mate with the queen.*

**Soldier** *Has enlarged head and jaws to help it defend the nest.*

**Worker** *Builds nests and looks for food.*

Most colonies have two main kinds of ants—the queen and female workers. There are only a few male ants in a nest and their only job is to mate with the queen. Soldier ants guard the nest.

**Special delivery** *Workers drop leaves at the entrance to the nest, where soldier ants stand guard.*

**Into the nest** *Workers carry the leaves into the nest.*

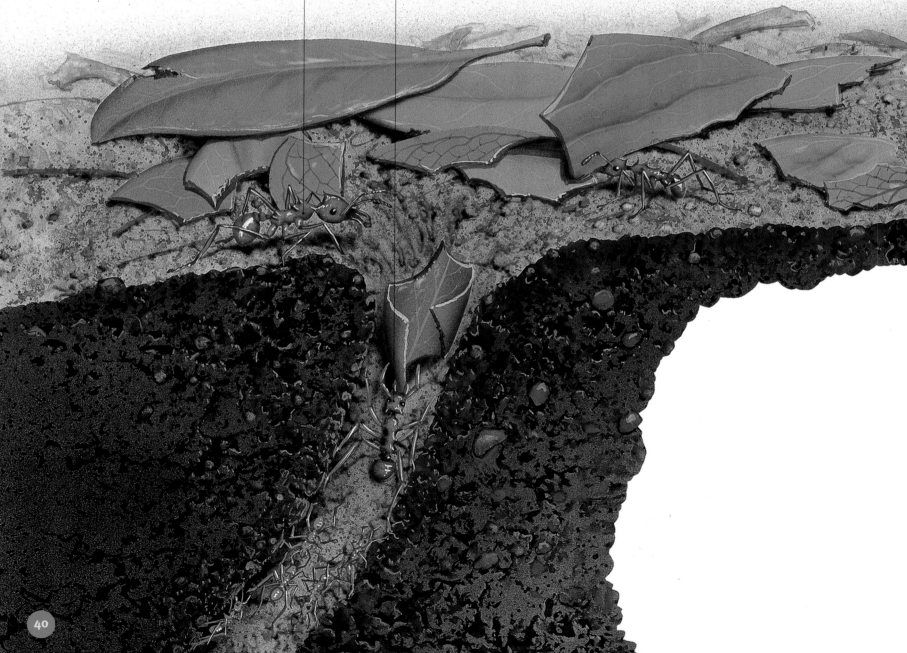

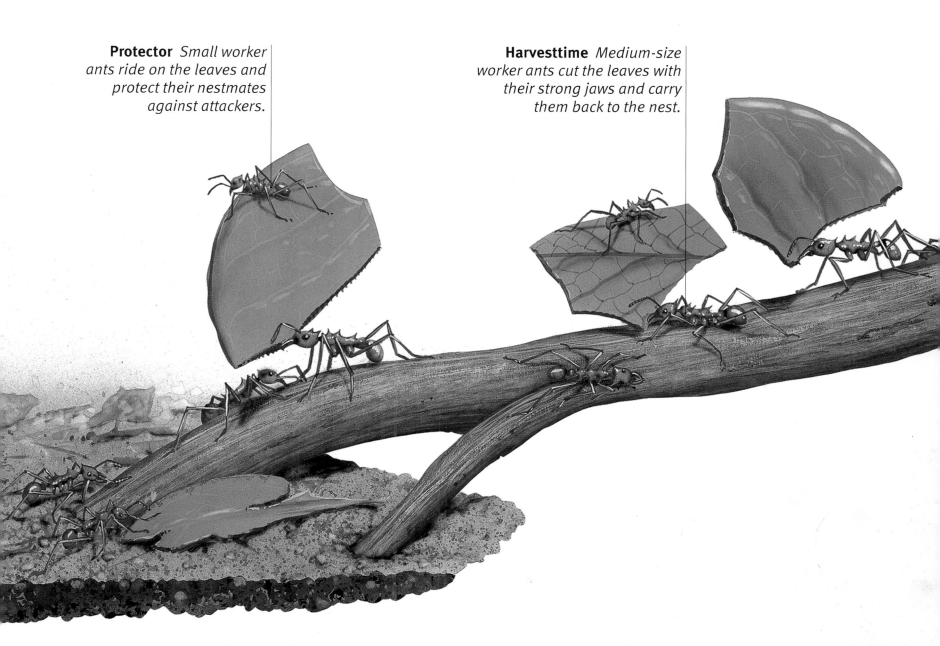

**Protector** *Small worker ants ride on the leaves and protect their nestmates against attackers.*

**Harvesttime** *Medium-size worker ants cut the leaves with their strong jaws and carry them back to the nest.*

# TEAM PLAYERS

Ants, wasps, and bees live and work together in organized colonies. There are around 10,000 species of ants and they are all social insects. Leaf-cutter ants work in teams to cut off leaves and take them back to the nest, guard them, chew them up, and, finally, use them as compost to grow their food—a special type of fungus. A mature leaf-cutter colony can house millions of ants.

# TERMITES

Termites are social insects. They build colonies, or nests, to live in. One colony can hold millions of termites, each with its own work to do—like other social insects, such as ants and bees. Most termite species live underground in colonies full of tunnels and chambers, which are used for different purposes. Some termites build their colonies aboveground and even in trees. They make special cement for tunnel walls by mixing their saliva with soil.

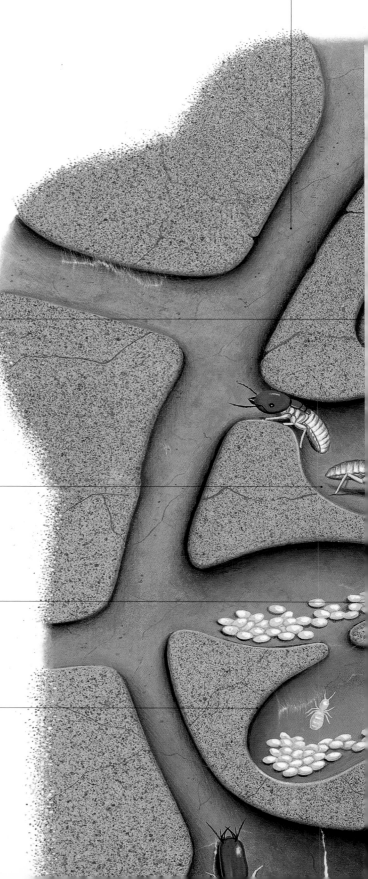

**Tunnels** *A maze of tunnels keeps air moving in the colony like an air-conditioning system.*

**Garden chamber**
*Fungus is grown here to provide food for the colony.*

**Workers' chamber**
*Surrounds the queen's chamber.*

**Queen's chamber**
*The queen can live for 15 years and lays millions of eggs.*

**Nursery chamber**
*Where eggs and nymphs are looked after.*

When a damp wood termite senses danger, it bangs its head on the tunnel walls. This makes vibrations, which warn other termites in the colony.

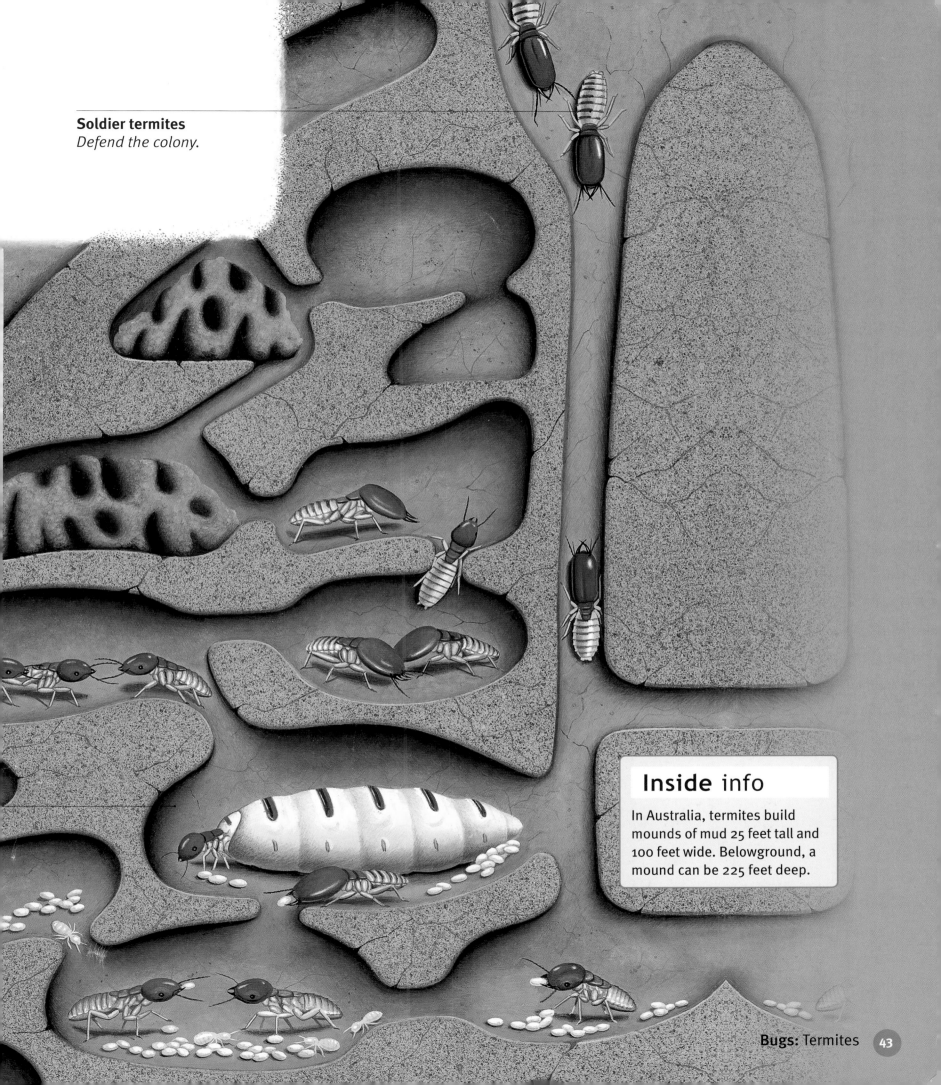

**Soldier termites**
*Defend the colony.*

## Inside info

In Australia, termites build mounds of mud 25 feet tall and 100 feet wide. Belowground, a mound can be 225 feet deep.

# BACKSWIMMERS

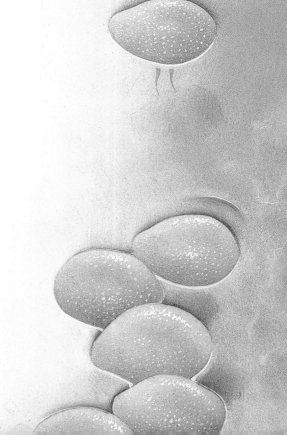

Many insects live in or around water. The backswimmer is one such bug—it lives in ponds and, as its name suggests, it swims upside down. The backswimmer has tiny hairs on its abdomen that catch an air bubble. The air is absorbed through little vents, or breathing holes. The backswimmer pounces on its food, stabs it with its sharp beak, and sucks up its juices. It can hunt and eat animals much larger than itself, such as tadpoles and small fish.

Insects use their legs for many different reasons. They use them to swim, walk, jump, and catch food. Each insect has legs that suit its needs.

**Protection** *This cricket leg is used for jumping and defense. It is covered in spikes and a tough armor.*

**Grasping** *Caterpillars have false legs with tiny hooks, which grip onto leaves and stems.*

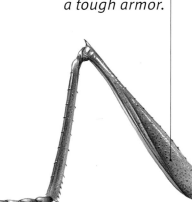

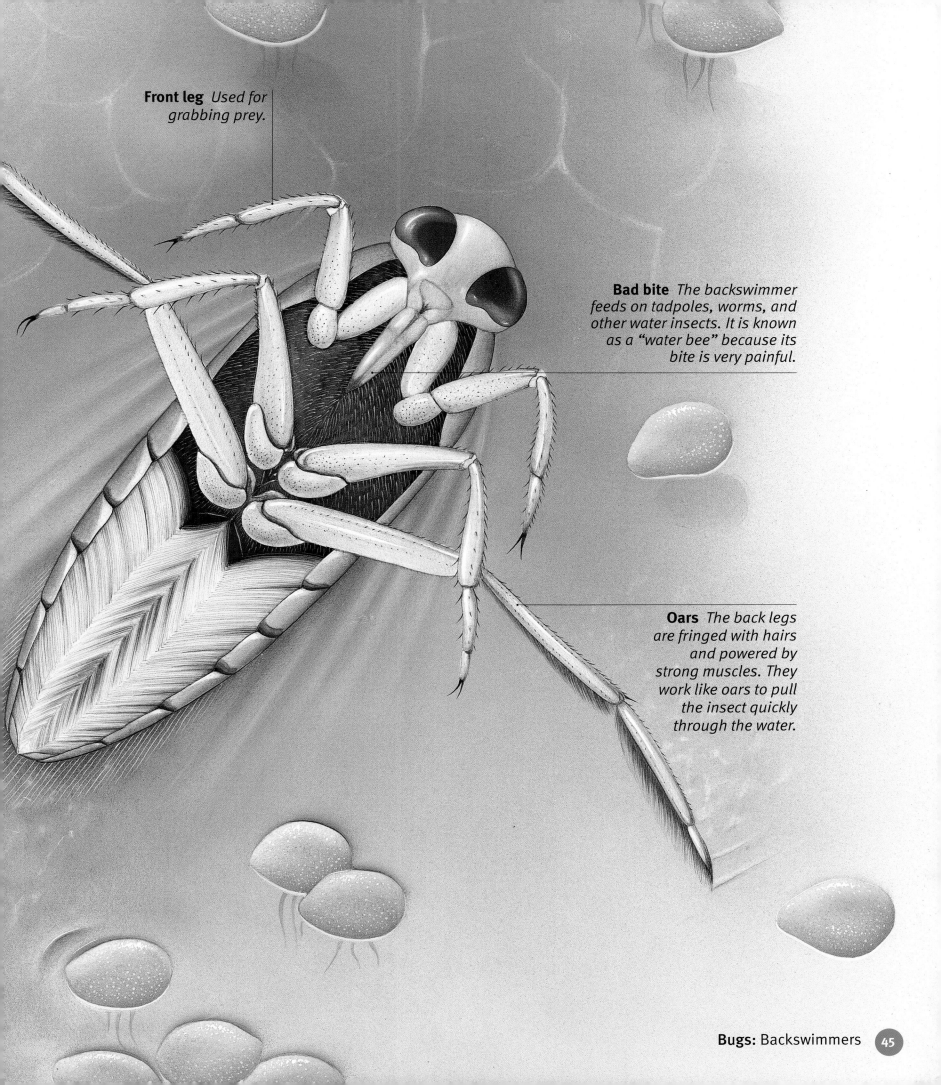

**Front leg** *Used for grabbing prey.*

**Bad bite** *The backswimmer feeds on tadpoles, worms, and other water insects. It is known as a "water bee" because its bite is very painful.*

**Oars** *The back legs are fringed with hairs and powered by strong muscles. They work like oars to pull the insect quickly through the water.*

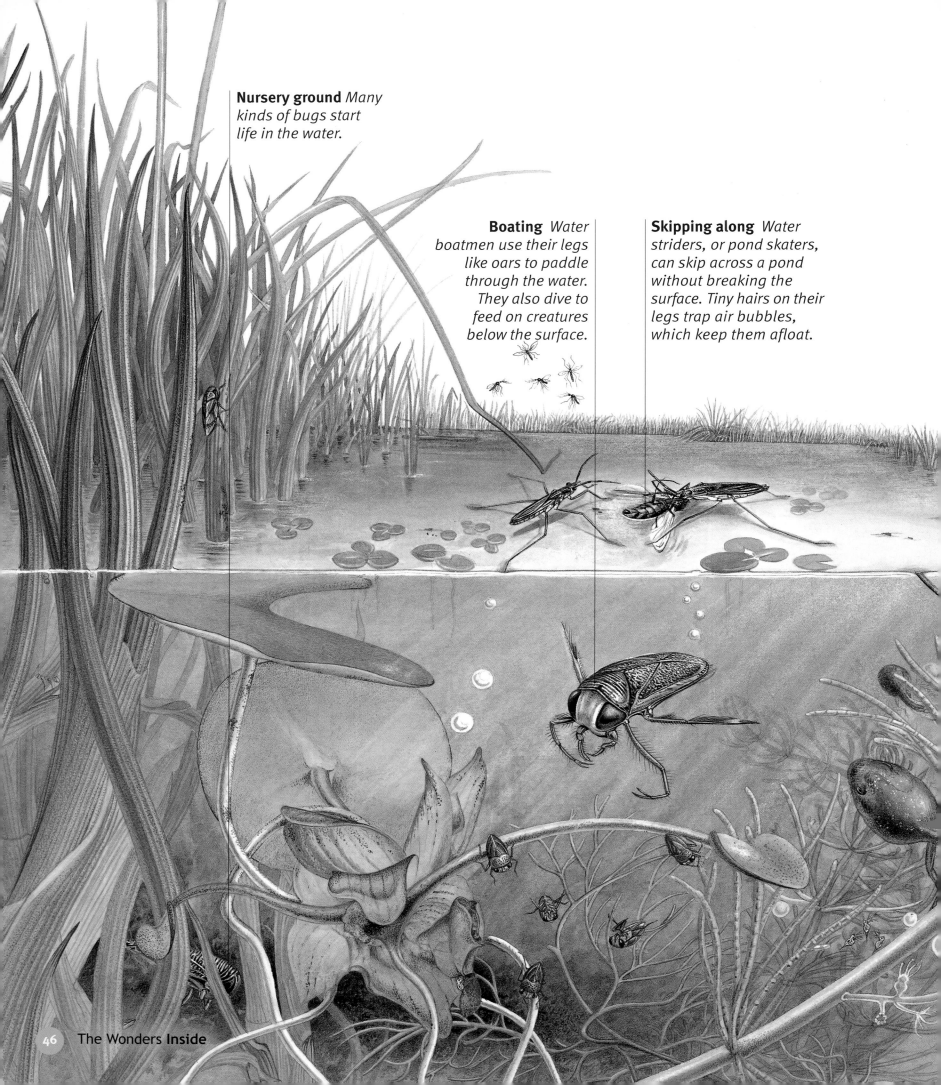

**Nursery ground** *Many kinds of bugs start life in the water.*

**Boating** *Water boatmen use their legs like oars to paddle through the water. They also dive to feed on creatures below the surface.*

**Skipping along** *Water striders, or pond skaters, can skip across a pond without breaking the surface. Tiny hairs on their legs trap air bubbles, which keep them afloat.*

# WATER WORLD

Many insects are aquatic, which means they live in the water. Aquatic insects need freshwater and can be found in ponds, lakes, and streams. Very few insects live in the sea. Insects that live in and around water have special body features that help them survive in their environment. Dragonflies are just one of many insects that start life underwater. Dragonfly nymphs move around by forcing water out through their abdomen, just like the jet engine on a boat.

**Hanging around**
*Water scorpions hang among the water weeds and wait to catch passing tadpoles with their powerful front legs.*

Insects that live underwater have to find ways to breathe in air.

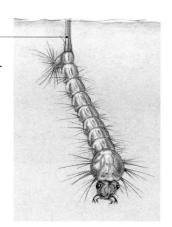

**Mosquito larvae**
*Hang underwater and have a tiny snorkel that connects their abdomen to the air above.*

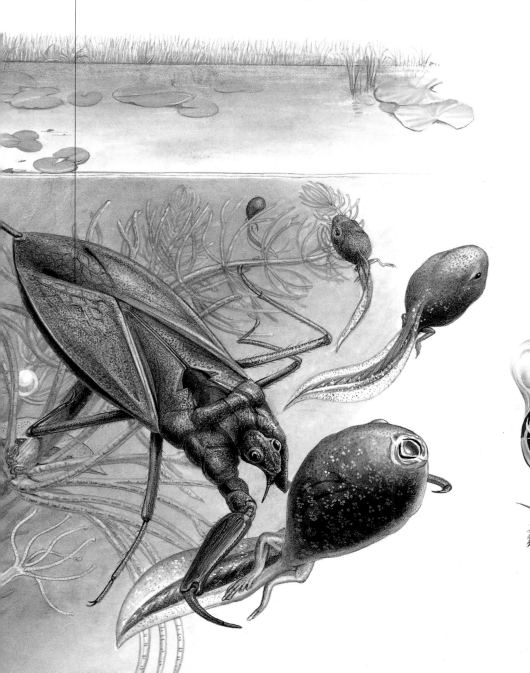

**Diving beetles** *Trap a bubble of air under their wing cases to make sure they can breathe underwater, just like a diver with air tanks.*

# PRAYING MANTISES

The praying mantis is the only insect that can turn its head around to look behind itself. Its compound eyes allow it to see movement from up to 60 feet away. It eats insects such as butterflies and grasshoppers, and sometimes bigger prey such as lizards and birds. A mantis waits and watches for a long time before it attacks. When ready, it shoots out its front legs in a surprise attack—it can shoot out and snatch passing prey in one-twentieth of a second. Then, legs gripped tightly around its prey, it starts eating with its strong jaws.

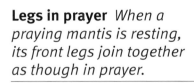

**Legs in prayer** *When a praying mantis is resting, its front legs join together as though in prayer.*

Like the praying mantis, the housefly and the assassin bug are hunters. The housefly turns its prey into liquid and then uses its proboscis to suck up this liquid. The assassin bug pierces its prey's skin and sucks it dry with its tubelike mouthpiece.

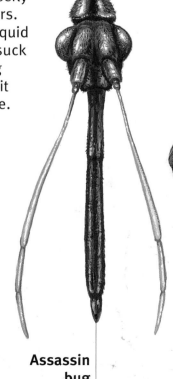

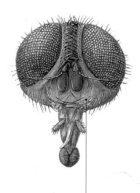

**Housefly**

**Assassin bug**

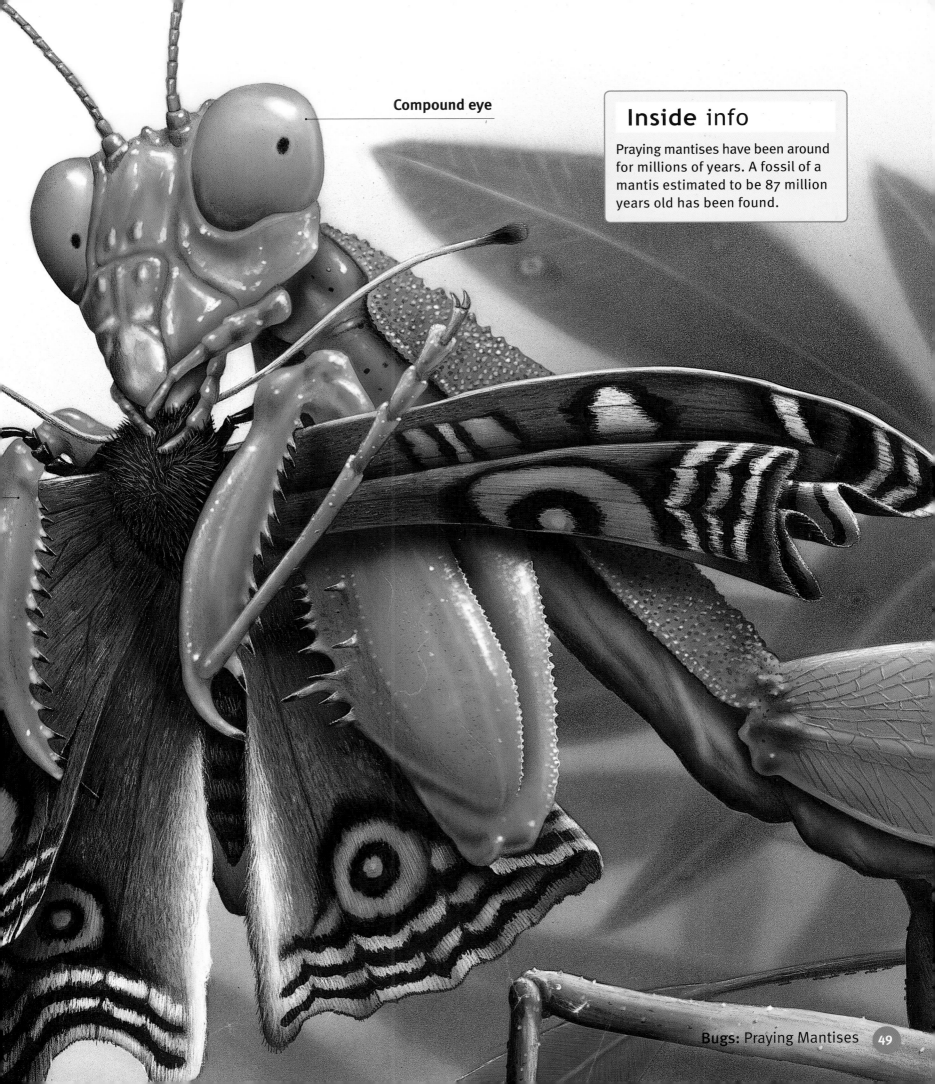

Compound eye

**Inside** info

Praying mantises have been around for millions of years. A fossil of a mantis estimated to be 87 million years old has been found.

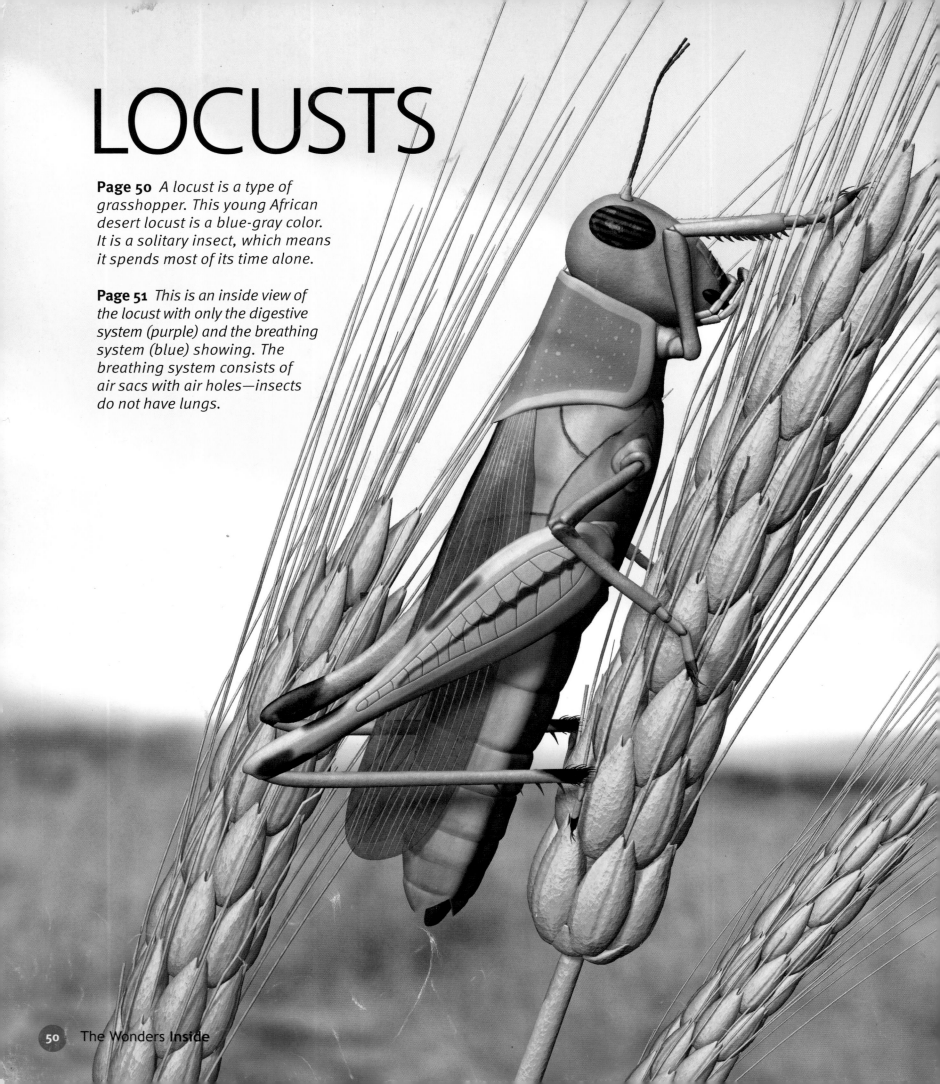

# LOCUSTS

**Page 50** *A locust is a type of grasshopper. This young African desert locust is a blue-gray color. It is a solitary insect, which means it spends most of its time alone.*

**Page 51** *This is an inside view of the locust with only the digestive system (purple) and the breathing system (blue) showing. The breathing system consists of air sacs with air holes—insects do not have lungs.*

**Page 52** *This inside view of the locust shows the circulatory system in pink and the nervous system in green, including the tiny brain in the head.*

**Page 53** *During favorable conditions, when there is plenty of food, the population of locusts increases. As they bump into each other, African desert locusts change to a yellow-brown color. They then swarm and form plagues.*

**Deadly deception**
*The orchid mantis sits very quietly, watching. When its prey, the grasshopper, is within striking distance, the mantis grabs it with its front legs.*

**Grasshopper**

**Flower**

# ORCHID MANTISES

The orchid mantis is a very rare insect. It eats moths, bees, butterflies, and even small lizards, and is itself hunted by lizards, birds, and spiders. The orchid mantis uses camouflage to trick both its prey and its predators. When it sits on a flower, it slowly changes color to become the same white or pink as the flower. It also has petal-shaped legs that make it look like a part of the flower. It is almost impossible to see. It keeps still and waits for its food to arrive—then it snaps its front legs shut and holds down its prey with sharp spines along its legs.

## Inside info

Insects are very good at mimicry, or copying, as a form of camouflage. Stick insects look exactly like parts of a tree. Sometimes this gets them into trouble. Other insects might nibble on them by mistake.

**Excess skin**
*The cicada nymph sheds its skin and emerges as a fully grown adult.*

## Inside info

In the United States there are two types of cicadas that live underground for 13 to 17 years. Incredibly, masses of them come out of the ground at exactly the same time. Nobody knows why they emerge all at once.

# CICADAS

Adult female cicadas lay their eggs in grooves cut into a twig. A nymph hatches from each egg and immediately buries itself in the soil. There it stays for two to five years, feeding on plant roots, growing, and shedding its skin. When it is almost fully grown, it tunnels out of the soil and sheds its skin one last time. Now it is an adult cicada. It will live long enough to attract a mate and breed.

**Making a racket** *Male cicadas are the loudest insects in the world. Muscles in their abdomen push on an organ called a tymbal. The tymbal pops in and out and makes a loud clicking sound that attracts females.*

The cicada nymph digs a tunnel to the surface when it is ready to emerge.

# WHAT IS A SPIDER?

Spiders belong to a group of animals called arachnids. Like insects, they have a tough outer shell, or exoskeleton. Unlike insects, spiders have two body parts, the cephalothorax and the abdomen. Spiders have eight legs and most also have eight eyes. On their jaws are two fangs, which can inject venom. All spiders release silk from the spinnerets on their abdomen, which they use to build webs. Spiders hear through tiny hairs on their legs, which pick up vibrations. Spiders usually eat insects and other spiders. Larger spiders may even eat fish and small mammals.

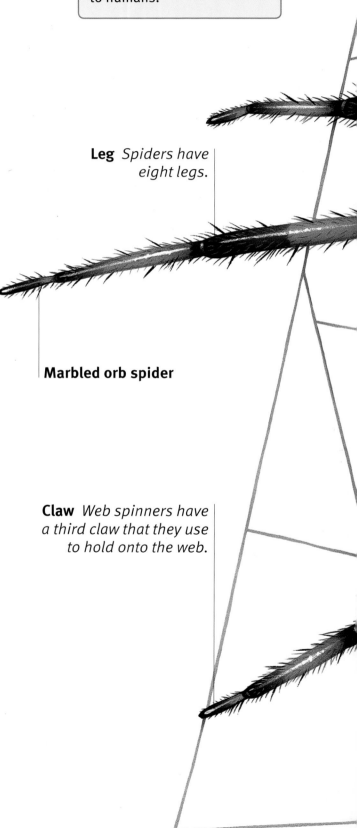

**Leg** *Spiders have eight legs.*

**Marbled orb spider**

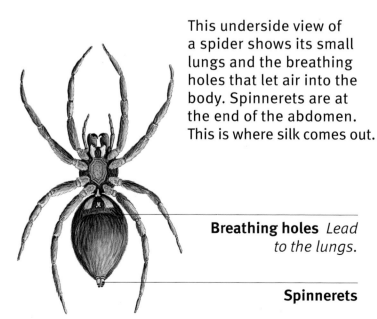

This underside view of a spider shows its small lungs and the breathing holes that let air into the body. Spinnerets are at the end of the abdomen. This is where silk comes out.

**Claw** *Web spinners have a third claw that they use to hold onto the web.*

**Breathing holes** *Lead to the lungs.*

**Spinnerets**

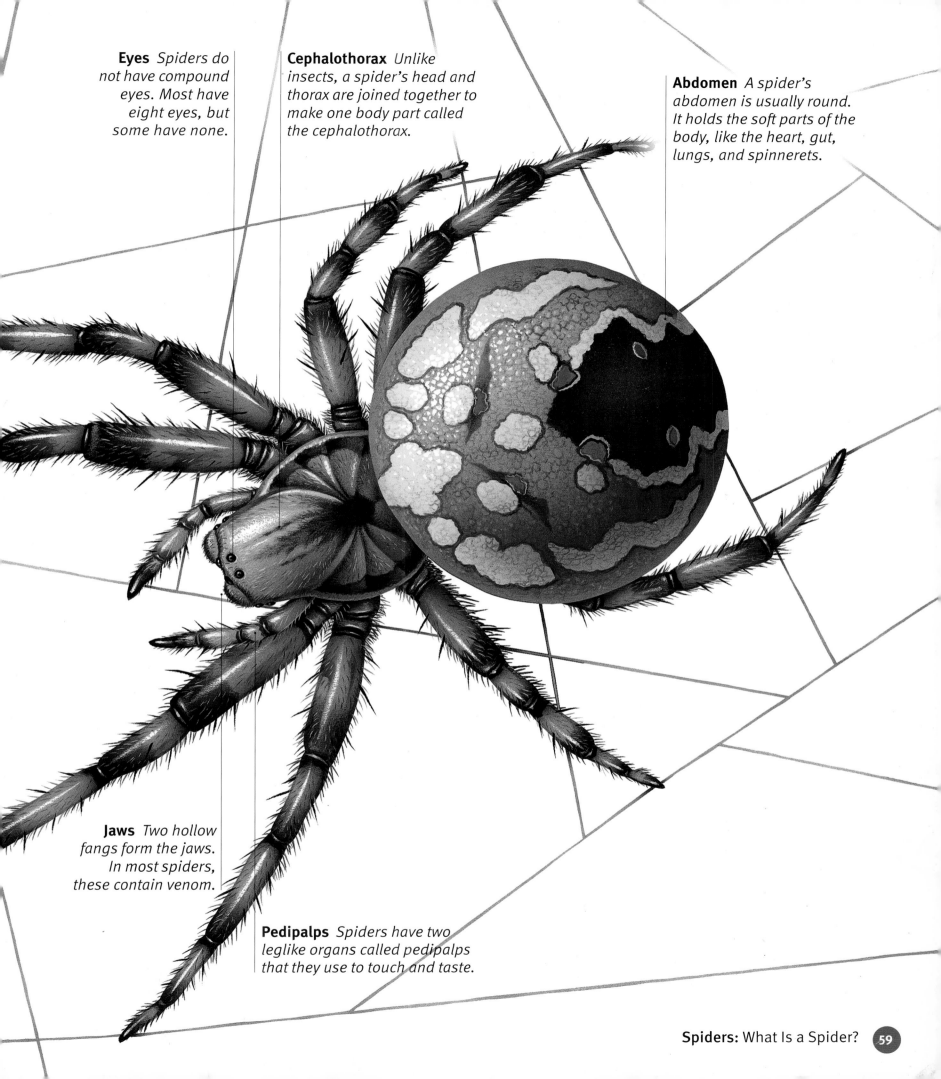

**Eyes** *Spiders do not have compound eyes. Most have eight eyes, but some have none.*

**Cephalothorax** *Unlike insects, a spider's head and thorax are joined together to make one body part called the cephalothorax.*

**Abdomen** *A spider's abdomen is usually round. It holds the soft parts of the body, like the heart, gut, lungs, and spinnerets.*

**Jaws** *Two hollow fangs form the jaws. In most spiders, these contain venom.*

**Pedipalps** *Spiders have two leglike organs called pedipalps that they use to touch and taste.*

# INSIDE A SPIDER

The inside of a spider's body is similar to the inside of many other animals. It has a brain, a heart, lungs, and a digestive system for breaking down food. The one thing that is different from most other animals is the spider's silk gland. Spiders use silk not only to make webs but also to wrap up their prey, wrap up their eggs, line burrows, and make draglines, trip wires, and sticky traps. Scientists say that spider silk could be the strongest material in the world. It is as strong as steel and as flexible as elastic.

## Inside info

Because spiders do not have sharp, biting mouthparts that can chew prey, all spiders partly digest or liquefy their food before swallowing.

**Ovary** *Produces eggs.*

**Heart** *Long, thin heart runs along the top of the abdomen.*

**Spinneret**

**Silk gland** *Produces silk, which is passed to the spinnerets.*

**Lung** *Major breathing organ.*

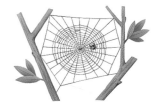

**First fork**          **Frame**          **Raylike threads**          **First spiral**          **Second spiral**

A spiderweb can be a carefully constructed network or a tangled mess. It depends on the spider. Some spiders build a new web every day; others just repair theirs. These drawings show the progression, from left to right, of a circular web. This is the kind of web garden spiders spin.

**Stomach** *Spiders have a sucking, muscular stomach.*

**Brain** *Control center of the body.*

**Venom gland** *Produces poison to kill prey or ward off attackers.*

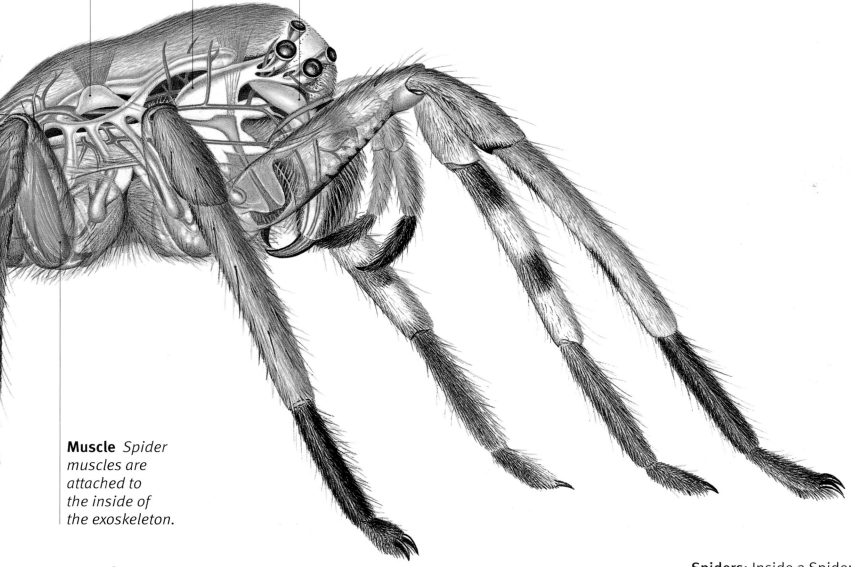

**Muscle** *Spider muscles are attached to the inside of the exoskeleton.*

# JUMPING SPIDERS

The jumping spider's eyesight is more powerful than that of any other spider. It has a large pair of eyes at the front, but it also has three pairs on the back of its cephalothorax. The eyes are arranged so the jumping spider can see in almost every direction at once. In addition to its excellent eyesight, the jumping spider has strong back legs that it uses to pounce on its prey. It can jump to a distance of 50 times its own body length. As it jumps, it spins a safety line that it uses to pull itself back. When it is time to mate, the male jumping spider waves his front legs in the air and does a special dance in front of the female.

**Female jumping spider**

Hunting spiders have powerful eyesight to help them find their prey. But spiders that sit in one place and wait for prey to come to them have weaker eyesight.

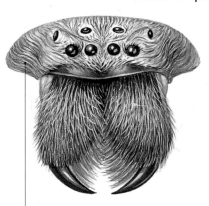

**Huntsman** *An active hunter. Its eyes are spread out in two rows so the spider can see better when looking for prey at night.*

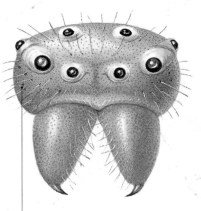

**Crab spider** *The small eyes of the crab spider sense the movement of prey. The spider attacks when the prey comes close enough.*

**Ogre-faced spider** *This spider has eight eyes, but two of them are enormous. It can hunt for prey in the dark.*

**Spiders:** Jumping Spiders 63

# WRITING SPIDERS

**64** *The writing spider eats insects, such as this [fly] that get caught in its sticky web. Writing spiders [lay their] eggs in a sac, called a cocoon, under nearby [leaves]. The cocoon is made of strong silk that protects [the] delicate eggs.*

**Page 65** *The writing spider has a special talent: it [makes] an X pattern in the center of its web, which [m]akes it firm. The pattern looks like scribble, which gives the spider its name. This view shows the eggs packed tightly inside the cocoon— they will hatch soon.*

**Page 66** *The abdomen of a spider contains large silk-producing glands. The strands of silk are squirted out from small nozzles, called spinnerets, which are at the tip of the abdomen. Here, the spiderlings have started to hatch.*

**Page 67** *Once the fly is trapped in the web, it is quickly injected with venom and wrapped in silk to be eaten later. The spiderlings have now hatched and have to fend for themselves.*

**Tarantula attack** *The Mexican
red-kneed tarantula rears up
and strikes at a passing lizard
with lightning speed.*

**Fangs**

# TARANTULAS

The tarantula eats lizards, frogs, mice, and even birds. It has very poor eyesight, so it uses sense organs on its legs to feel the vibrations that these creatures make as they pass by. It either sits and waits for them to cross its path, or it hunts them down. When the tarantula is ready to strike, it lifts its body up, raises its fangs, and lunges at its prey.

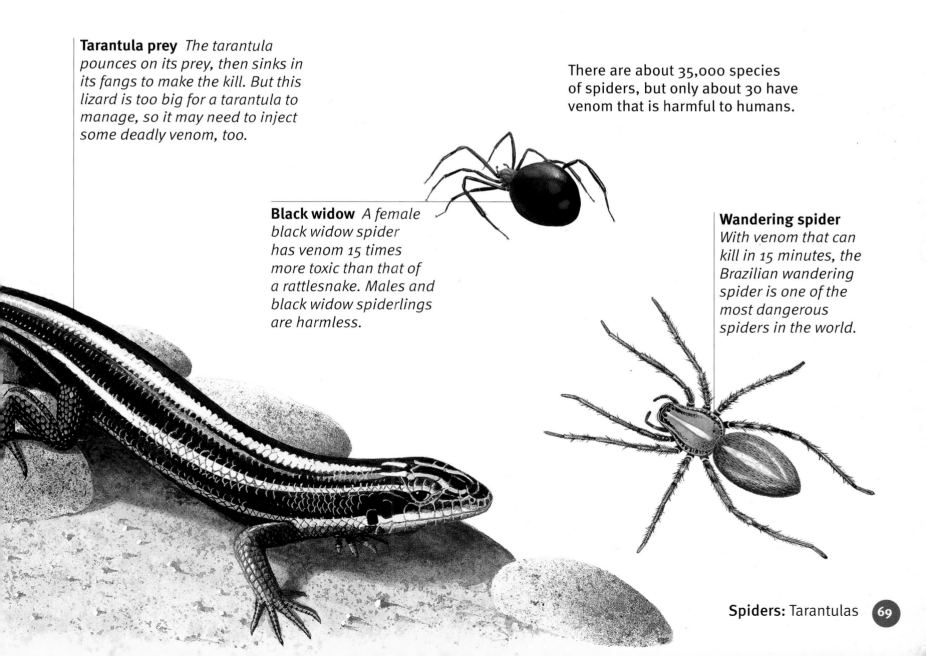

**Tarantula prey** *The tarantula pounces on its prey, then sinks in its fangs to make the kill. But this lizard is too big for a tarantula to manage, so it may need to inject some deadly venom, too.*

There are about 35,000 species of spiders, but only about 30 have venom that is harmful to humans.

**Black widow** *A female black widow spider has venom 15 times more toxic than that of a rattlesnake. Males and black widow spiderlings are harmless.*

**Wandering spider** *With venom that can kill in 15 minutes, the Brazilian wandering spider is one of the most dangerous spiders in the world.*

# REDBACK SPIDERS

The redback spider is found all over Australia. It lives under rocks and logs in dry forests and deserts, as well as in dry, sheltered spots in house roofs, sheds, and gardens. The female's shiny black body has red markings on the belly and a red or orange stripe running down the back. The male is more brown, with dull red or white markings. It is half the size of the female, and is too small for its bite to harm people. But the female's bite can kill a person who is not treated with antivenin. Fortunately, the redback is shy and slow—most bites happen when a person touches one by accident.

**Redback food**  *Insects, especially ground dwellers, are the most common prey. But sometimes, redback spiders trap and eat small lizards and mice.*

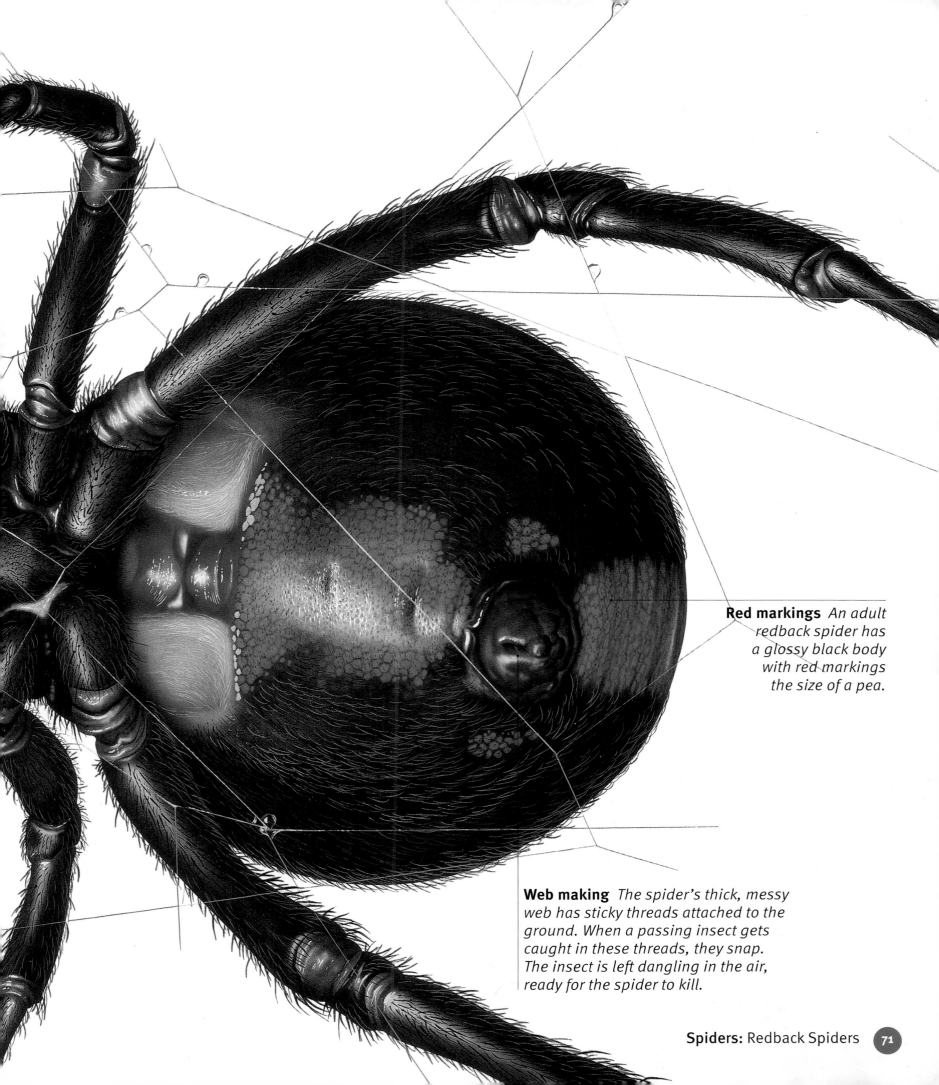

**Red markings** *An adult redback spider has a glossy black body with red markings the size of a pea.*

**Web making** *The spider's thick, messy web has sticky threads attached to the ground. When a passing insect gets caught in these threads, they snap. The insect is left dangling in the air, ready for the spider to kill.*

# TRAPDOOR SPIDERS

Spiders have many predators, such as birds, lizards, and small mammals. They have developed different ways to defend themselves. Some hide, some drop out of their webs and escape, and others disguise themselves to look like more dangerous animals. The trapdoor spider builds a secret chamber underground, at the bottom of a burrow. The chamber has a door that the spider can pull shut to keep predators out.

Crab spiders change color to match whatever flower they are sitting on. This hides them from enemies and also from prey such as honeybees.

**Giant centipede** *A predator finds the burrow and enters.*

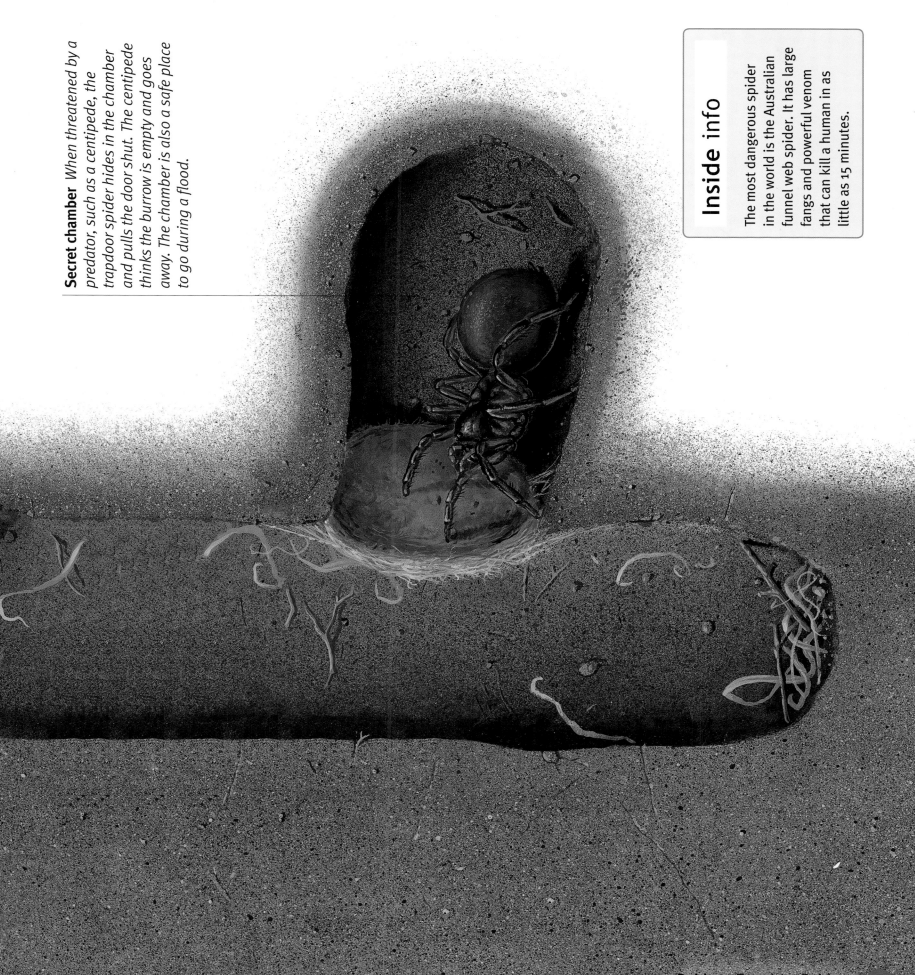

**Secret chamber** *When threatened by a predator, such as a centipede, the trapdoor spider hides in the chamber and pulls the door shut. The centipede thinks the burrow is empty and goes away. The chamber is also a safe place to go during a flood.*

## Inside info

The most dangerous spider in the world is the Australian funnel web spider. It has large fangs and powerful venom that can kill a human in as little as 15 minutes.

# INSECT EATERS

It is not only animal attackers that insects and spiders have to watch out for. There are also some plants that can catch and eat insects and spiders. These plants are meat-eaters, or carnivores. They lure insects and spiders with nectar and bright colors, but trap and kill them instead, then they use special juices to digest them.

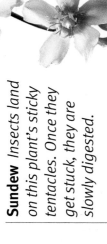

**Sundew** Insects land on this plant's sticky tentacles. Once they get stuck, they are slowly digested.

**Pitcher plant** *Bright colors and nectar on the lips of its leaves lure insects to this plant. The insect slides down a slippery inner wall into the plant's digestive juices. There it is broken down and absorbed as food.*

**Venus flytrap** *A fly is lured by the bright colors and sweet juices of the Venus flytrap. Once inside the trap of open red leaves, it brushes against the plant's sensitive hairs. This triggers the trap to snap shut, and the fly is then digested.*

# WHAT IS A BEETLE?

There are more than 400,000 kinds of beetles, and new ones are being discovered all the time. Beetles make up almost half of all insects and a third of all animals on earth. All beetles have a very thick outer shell, or exoskeleton, which acts like body armor. They have a pair of hardened front wings. These form a case that protects the delicate back wings underneath. Beetles have powerful jaws for biting and chewing. They eat plants and sometimes other insects.

Beetles come in all shapes, sizes, and colors. They are found in all places on the earth—except in the sea and in the polar regions.

**Bee-eating beetle**
*Brightly colored to trick attackers into thinking it is dangerous.*

**South American longhorn beetle** *Uses its antennae to locate a mate more than 2 miles away.*

**African jewel beetle**
*Has tufts of hair that let it blend into its surroundings.*

**Jaws** *Mouthparts are like pincers and are used to grab and cut food.*

**Extra-thick exoskeleton**
*A beetle's exoskeleton is made up of many tiny plates called sclerites. These are tough but also bend so the beetle can move easily.*

**Protective wing case** *Flying beetles' wings are kept folded under wing cases when they are not in use. These cases are called elytra. In beetles that do not fly, the elytra are joined together to form extra body armor.*

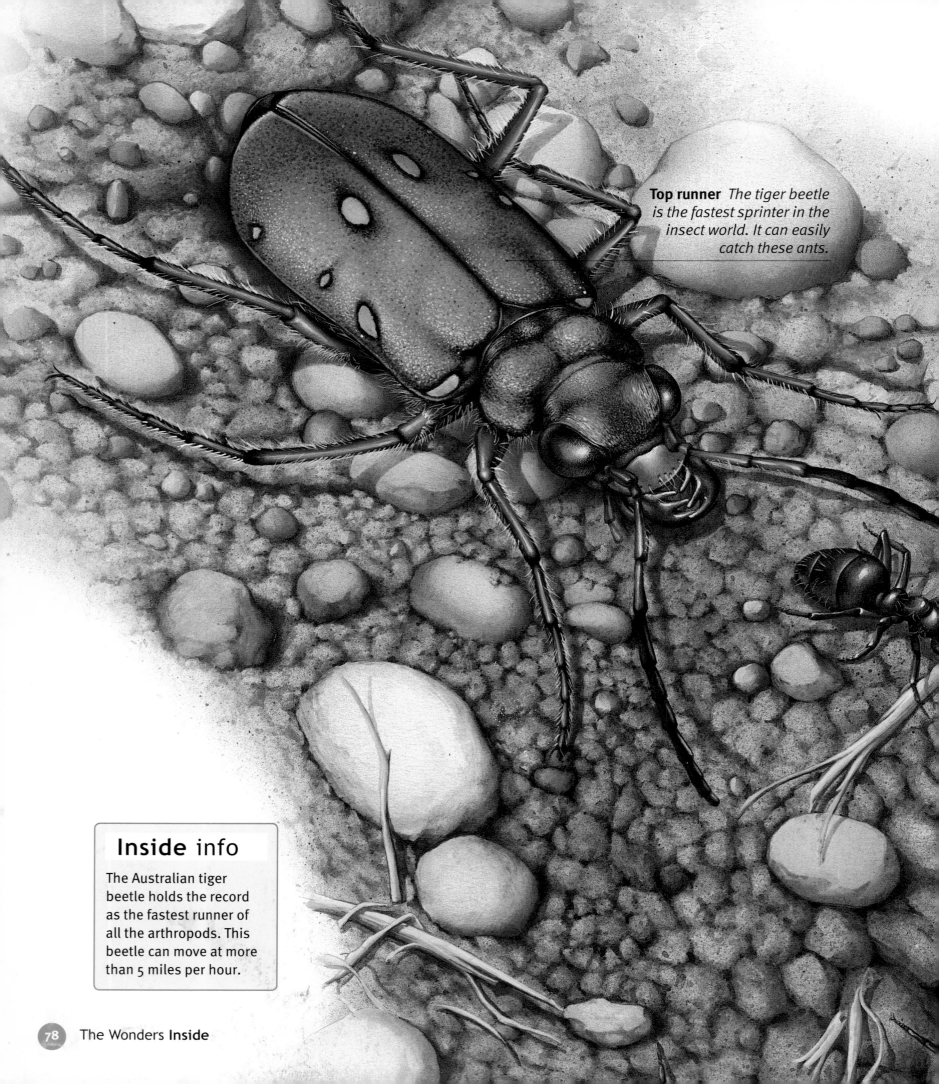

**Top runner** *The tiger beetle is the fastest sprinter in the insect world. It can easily catch these ants.*

## Inside info

The Australian tiger beetle holds the record as the fastest runner of all the arthropods. This beetle can move at more than 5 miles per hour.

# TIGER BEETLES

The tiger beetle is one of the greatest hunters of the beetle family. It eats other insects, such as grasshoppers, crickets, ants, flies, and even other beetles. It is so named because of the way it hunts its prey. It uses its huge, keen eyes to sense surrounding movement. Once it has spotted food, its strong, fast legs enable it to outrun its prey. Finally, the tiger beetle uses its razor-sharp jaws to kill and eat its prey.

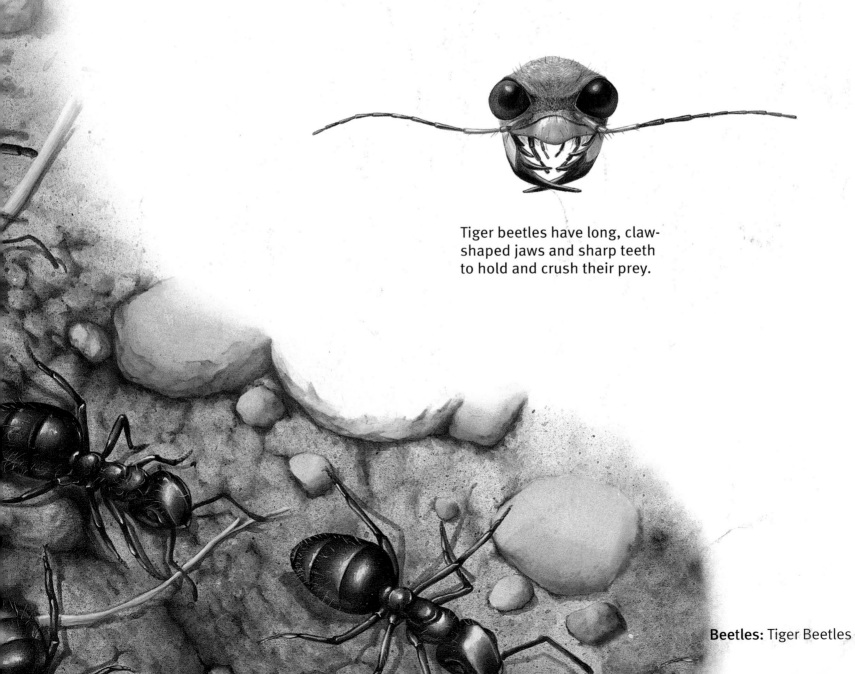

Tiger beetles have long, claw-shaped jaws and sharp teeth to hold and crush their prey.

**Safe landing** *After a flea beetle jumps, it always lands on its feet, and it also lands exactly where it wants. It can also walk and fly.*

When an insect walks, it moves three legs at once: the first and third leg on one side and the middle leg on the other side. Then the other three legs step out. This produces a zigzag walk.

# FLEA BEETLES

Not all insects fly to get around. Some walk, some wriggle, and some jump. The flea beetle is a small jumping beetle. It has an extra-large thighbone in its back legs with a special organ designed for jumping. When the flea beetle is touched or surprised, this organ acts like a spring and launches the beetle into the air. It spins end over end at speeds of more than 9 miles an hour. As it falls, it turns up to 70 somersaults in just one second.

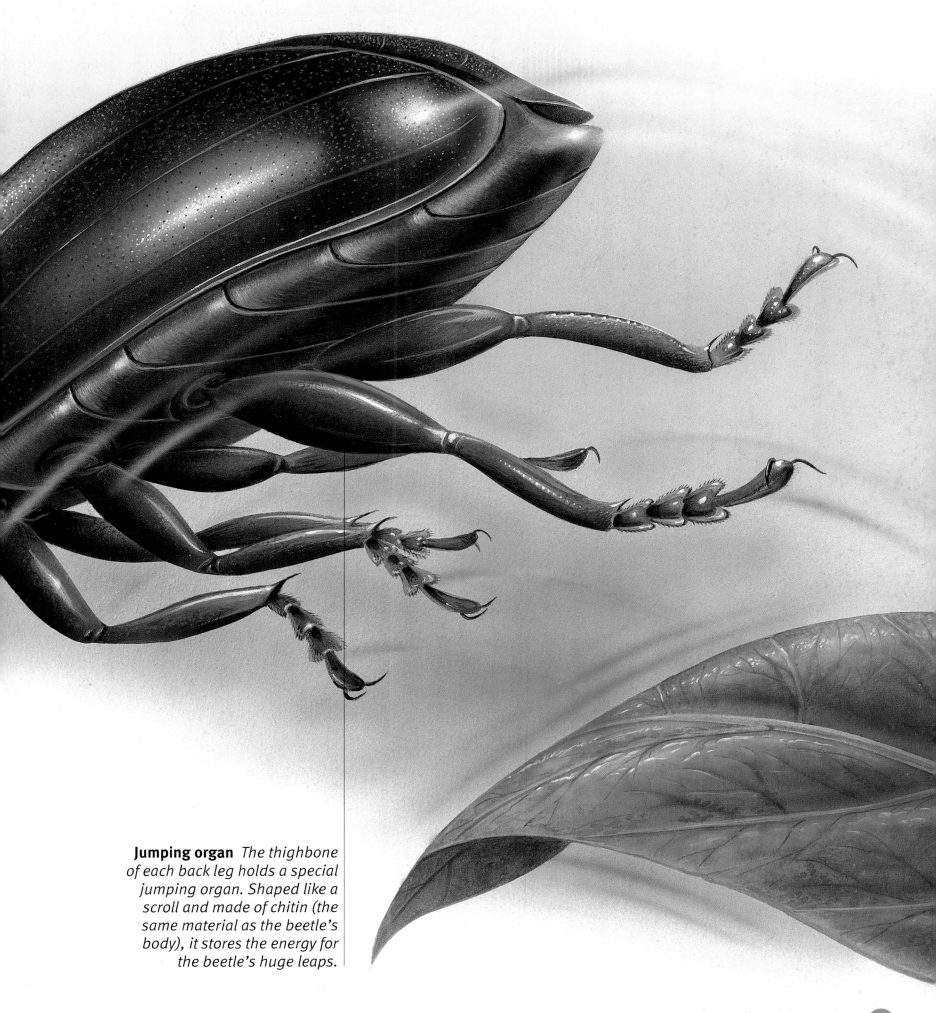

**Jumping organ** *The thighbone of each back leg holds a special jumping organ. Shaped like a scroll and made of chitin (the same material as the beetle's body), it stores the energy for the beetle's huge leaps.*

# LADYBUGS

There are more than 5,000 kinds of ladybugs. They are easily recognized by their brightly colored and spotted wing covers. These wing covers, called elytra, are hardened front wings. They form a case that covers and protects the delicate back wings when the ladybug is not flying. Ladybugs are often red, orange, or yellow with black spots. These spots fade as the bug gets older. They feed on plants and small insects, such as mites and plant lice. Farmers like ladybugs because they eat many of the insects that destroy their crops.

When not flying, the ladybug folds its back wings away under its spotted wing cases.

When getting ready to fly, the ladybug opens its wing cases and unfolds its back wings.

## Inside info

At the end of summer, huge groups of ladybugs swarm together to look for a place to hibernate, or sleep, during the winter months.

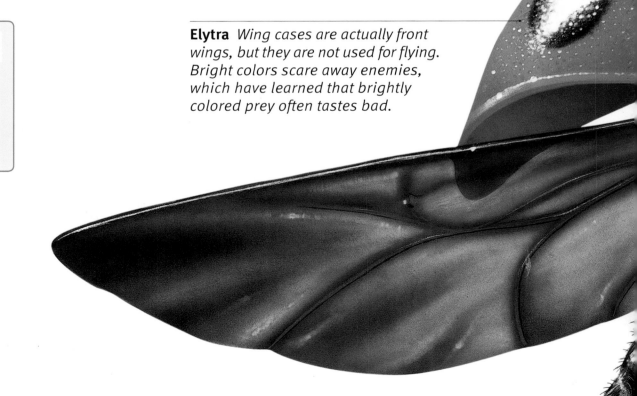

**Elytra** *Wing cases are actually front wings, but they are not used for flying. Bright colors scare away enemies, which have learned that brightly colored prey often tastes bad.*

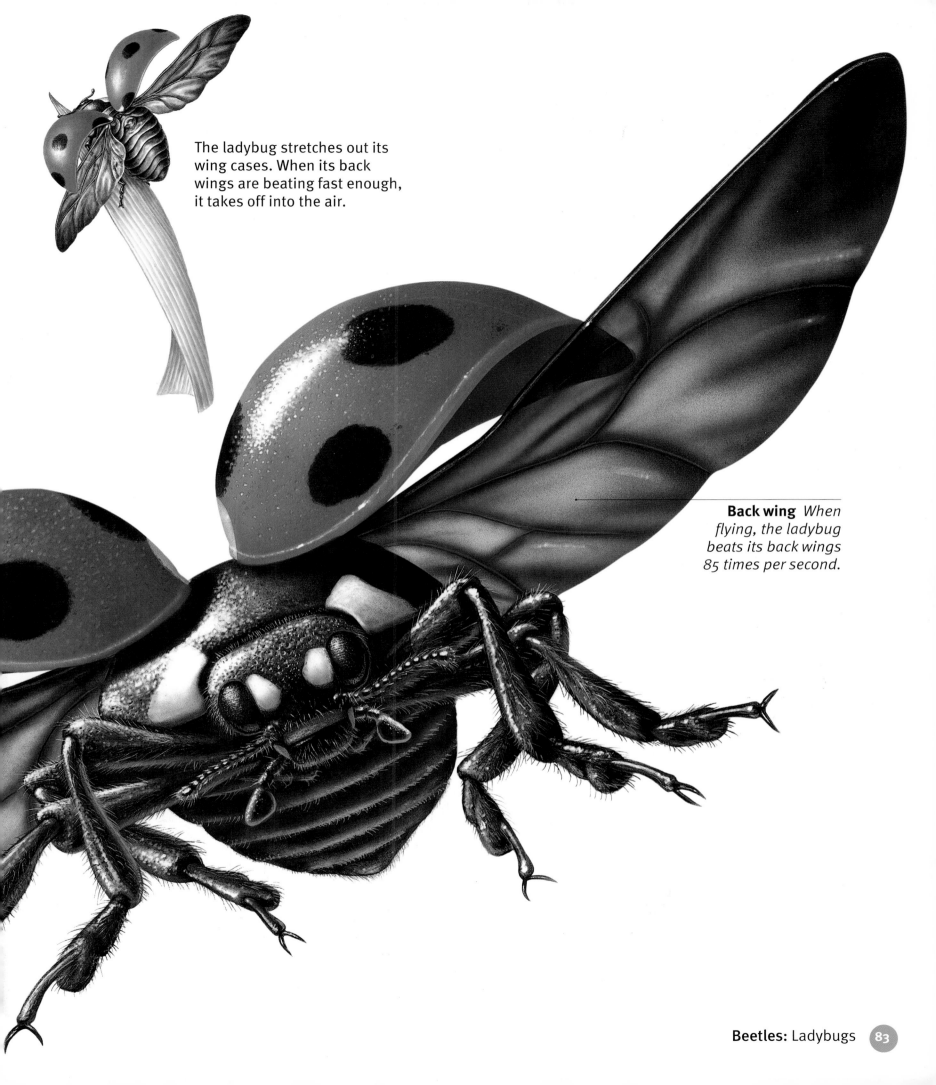

The ladybug stretches out its wing cases. When its back wings are beating fast enough, it takes off into the air.

**Back wing** *When flying, the ladybug beats its back wings 85 times per second.*

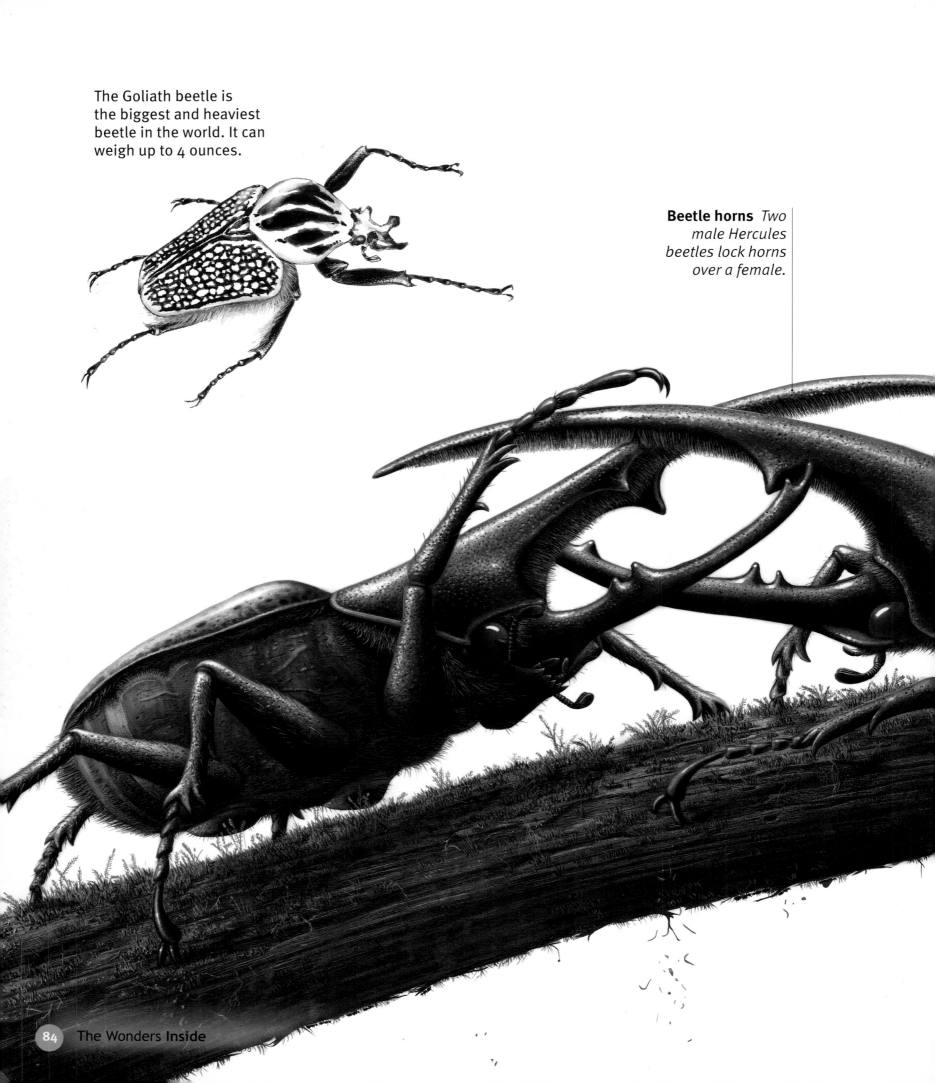

The Goliath beetle is the biggest and heaviest beetle in the world. It can weigh up to 4 ounces.

**Beetle horns** *Two male Hercules beetles lock horns over a female.*

# HERCULES BEETLES

The plant-eating Hercules beetle is the strongest beetle in the world. It can pick up objects 850 times its own weight. The male Hercules beetle uses two enormous curved horns to fight other beetles, either for the attentions of a female or for food. The two beetles try to pick each other up with their horns and toss their opponent to the ground. Although they look dangerous, the horns rarely cause permanent damage and one of the beetles usually runs away.

**Female Hercules beetle**
*This female waits to see which male Hercules beetle will win the fight. Females do not have horns.*

# DUNG BEETLES

Dung beetles eat the droppings of animals such as cows, sheep, deer, and elephants. They can eat more than their own weight in dung in a single day. This makes these beetles very important, because they keep the environment from being covered with animal manure. Dung beetles fly for miles, directed by their strong sense of smell, in search of fresh dung. When they find it, some types of dung beetles form it into balls that can be as big as apples. A male and female work together, rolling the ball back to their burrow. There, they squeeze the dung through their mouthparts and drink the liquid. The female also lays her eggs in the ball. When the larvae hatch, they eat the dung that surrounds them before eventually breaking out of the ball.

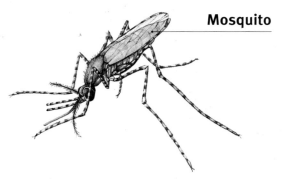

**Mosquito**

Insects can both help and harm humans. One type of mosquito carries malaria in its salivary glands and injects it into people when it bites them. This disease kills between two and four million people every year.

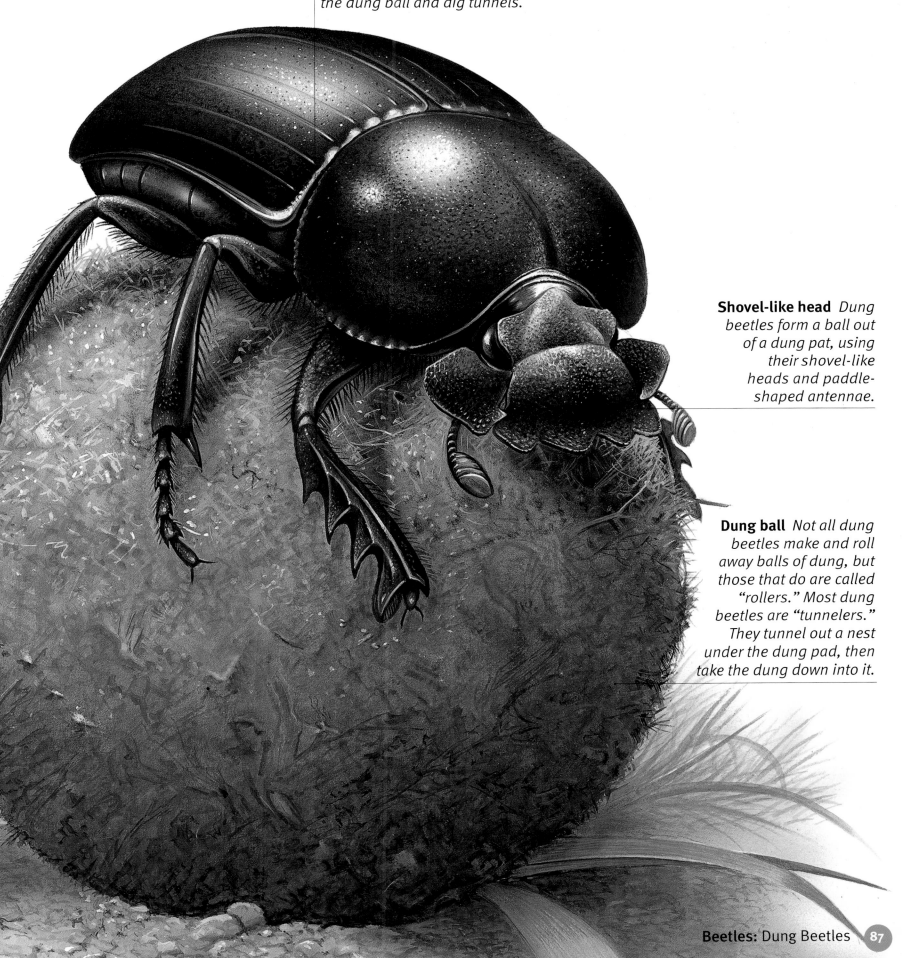

**Toothed legs** *Front legs are toothed, to help the beetle grip the dung ball and dig tunnels.*

**Shovel-like head** *Dung beetles form a ball out of a dung pat, using their shovel-like heads and paddle-shaped antennae.*

**Dung ball** *Not all dung beetles make and roll away balls of dung, but those that do are called "rollers." Most dung beetles are "tunnelers." They tunnel out a nest under the dung pad, then take the dung down into it.*

# GLOSSARY

**ABDOMEN**
The hind part of the body of an insect or spider that contains the digestive, respiratory, circulatory, and reproductive organs.

**ANTENNAE**
Long, thin sense organs on an insect's head that it uses to smell, touch, and hear.

**AQUATIC INSECTS**
Insects that live in water for all or most of their lives.

**ARACHNID**
A type of arthropod with eight walking legs, such as spiders, scorpions, mites, and ticks.

**ARTHROPOD**
An animal with jointed legs and a hard exoskeleton. There are many different types of arthropods, including insects, spiders, centipedes, millipedes, crabs, and lobsters. Arthropods make up about 90 percent of the animal kingdom.

**CAMOUFLAGE**
The colors or patterns of an insect that hide it from predators. They blend in with the surrounding environment so that it is hard to see them.

**CARNIVORE**
An animal that feeds on other animals.

**CEPHALOTHORAX**
The front part of a spider that combines the head and thorax. The legs and mouthparts are attached to it, and the spider's stomach, venom glands, and brain are all found inside. It is protected by a hard exoskeleton.

**CHITIN**
The strong material of an arthropod's exoskeleton.

**CIRCULATORY SYSTEM**
The organs that carry blood around the body. Insects do not use their blood to transport oxygen, so their blood is not red like mammals' blood—it is colorless.

**COCOON**
The protective case surrounding the eggs of spiders and the pupa of some insects. It is often made of silk.

**COLONY**
A group of closely related animals that work and live together in a nest, mound, or hive, such as ants, bees, wasps, and termites.

**COMPOUND EYE**
An eye that is made from hundreds, or even thousands, of smaller eyes, each with its own lens. Compound eyes can be found among insects and some crustaceans.

**DIGESTIVE SYSTEM**
The system of the body that is responsible for the digestion of food.

**DRAGLINE**
A strand of silk that a spider drags behind it as it builds its web or looks for food. If the spider has to drop from its web, it uses the dragline to climb back home again.

**DRONE**
A male wasp or bee that is larger than the workers and smaller than the queen. Its role in the hive is to fertilize the queen. It dies shortly afterward.

**ELYTRA**
The hard, tough front wings of a beetle that cover and protect the delicate flying wings beneath.

**EXOSKELETON**
The hard outer skeleton that supports the muscles and protects the soft organs inside an insect's body. The exoskeleton does not grow with the insect, so when it gets too tight, the insect sheds or molts the exoskeleton and grows another.

**GRUBS**
The larvae of ants, bees, wasps, and beetles. Usually grubs have no legs, but some wasps and beetles have larvae with legs that make them look like caterpillars.

**HALTERES**
The club-shaped wings of flies, mosquitoes, and midges that help them to maintain balance when flying.

## LARVA

The young stage of many animals, including insects. They undergo a transformation called metamorphosis, when they change into adult form. Caterpillars, grubs, and maggots are all larval insects.

## METAMORPHOSIS

The process of changing into the adult form. In many insects, this change is very dramatic and is called "complete metamorphosis," such as when a caterpillar becomes a butterfly. Some insects change only slightly and go through a process called "incomplete metamorphosis," such as when a nymph becomes an adult.

## MIMICRY

Some animals resemble another animal in color and body shape in order to survive. Insects and spiders often have markings on their bodies that make them look like other animals. This fools predators into thinking they are poisonous or dangerous when they are not.

## NECTAR

A sweet liquid made by plants to attract animals, particularly insects and birds, that then transfer pollen from one flower to another.

## NERVOUS SYSTEM

Insects have sense organs, such as antennae and eyes, that help them detect what is happening around them. Nerves act as pathways and carry signals back and forth between the insects' sense organs and the brain. These work together to form the nervous system.

## NYMPH

A young insect that looks somewhat like its parents. They undergo incomplete metamorphosis when transforming into the adult insect.

## OCELLI

These simple eyes cannot form an image but are sensitive to the direction and intensity of light.

## PEDIPALPS

Spiders have two leglike sense organs called pedipalps that they use to touch, taste, and smell. Male spiders use them to mate.

## PREDATOR

An animal that hunts and eats other animals.

## PROBOSCIS

A tubelike mouthpart that insects, such as butterflies and moths, use like a straw to suck up liquid food.

## PROLEGS

The extra legs that caterpillars have on their abdomen to provide a firm grip on the leaves and stems of plants.

## PUPA

The stage in the life of many insects when the larva changes into an adult.

## SILK

A very light but strong, elastic thread that is made by spiders and some other insects. Spiders use it to build webs, catch food, line burrows, wrap prey, form cocoons, and produce draglines.

## SOCIAL INSECT

An insect that lives and works cooperatively with other insects of the same kind.

## SPINNERETS

Turrets found at the tip of a spider's abdomen, from which threads of silk are ejected.

## STYLET

A sharp mouthpart used to stab prey.

## THORAX

The middle part of an insect's body. It contains the muscles that power the insect's legs and wings.

## TYMBALS

A pair of special sound-producing organs found at the base of a cicada's abdomen. Muscles cause a drum to vibrate to produce the loud sound used by males to attract females.

## VENOM

A poison that is injected into another animal to kill or paralyze it.

## WORKER

A common social insect, such as certain ants, bees, wasps, or termites, that collects food and looks after the young in a colony.

# INDEX

# CREDITS

The publisher thanks Lachlan McLaine, Jen Taylor, and Shan Wolody for their contributions, and Puddingburn for the index.

Key t=top; tl=top left; tr=top right; b=bottom; bl=bottom left; br=bottom right; c=center; cr=center right

**ILLUSTRATIONS**
**Front cover** The Art Agency (Sandra Pond)
**Back cover** The Art Agency (Sandra Doyle) tr; Simone End bl; Christer Eriksson br; MBA Studios c; Trevor Ruth tl
**Spine** Simone End
**Endpapers** Sarah Norton
**The Art Agency (Robin Carter)** 12–15; **(Sandra Doyle)** 8bl; 24–25, 46–47, 60–61, 62–63; **(Ian Jackson)** 20–21, 32tl bl; **(Sandra Pond)** 36–39; **(Steve Roberts)** 10–11, 44b, 76b, 80–81,

86–87; **(Chris Shields)** 34tr, 42bl, 68–69; **Anne Bowman** 69c, 79c; **Contact Jupiter (Yvan Meunier)** 74–75; **Simone End** 18 bc br, 82tr, 83tl; **Christer Eriksson** 8–9, 48–49, 82–83, 84–85; **Jon Gittoes** 44–45; **Ray Grinaway** 8b, 30bl, 42–43, 72tr, 76–77; **Steve Hobbs** 50–53, 56–57; **Frank Knight** 11b; **MagicGroup** 84tl; **Rob Mancini** 16b, 18–19, 58–59, 61t; **MBA Studios** 34–35; **James McKinnon** 18bl, 54–55, 72–73; **Trevor Ruth** 16–17, 30–31; **Claudia Saraceni** 78–79, 86bl; **Kevin Stead** 22–23, 32–33, 40–41, 47b cr, 70–71; **Thomas Trojer** 58bl